FIRED UP VEGETARIAN

NO NONSENSE BARBECUING

FIRED UP
VEGETARIAN
NO NONSENSE BARBECUING
ROSS DOBSON

MURDOCH BOOKS

CONTENTS

INTRODUCTION

When looking for vegetarian recipes for inspiration, you really don't have to search too hard: next time you are at your local South-East Asian, Chinese, Indian, Japanese or Middle Eastern restaurant, have a closer look at the menu. These cultures have long traditions of vegetarianism, so naturally their cuisines are loaded with wonderful vegetarian dishes, featuring ingredients that are now more easily accessible than ever before.

I happen to be Australian, and in Australia we do love our barbecues. And many vegetarian dishes from afar are indeed perfectly suited to barbecuing. But I must be a little careful here, as this is no more an Australian cookbook than it is a cookbook just for vegetarians.

Vegetarian barbecue cookery is not about trying to reinvent the wheel. And good vegetarian cooking is certainly not about a need to make a meat substitute. Some vegetarian dishes stand alone as marvels in their own right. The famous Middle Eastern eggplant (aubergine) dip known as baba ghanoush, for instance, simply cannot be made without a good lick from a naked flame. This purplish black vegetable (well, actually, it's a fruit) withstands the searing heat of the barbecue, while the flesh inside cooks to a silky, smoke-infused softness.

Or how about barbecued onion rings, which often start off the barbecue because they take some time to slowly cook to a soft, golden, caramelised sweetness, filling the air with a mouthwatering fug, while also seasoning the hotplate nicely, ready to flavour the next batch of barbecued food. Barbecued onions are good enough to eat on their own, but toss them warm, into a bowl with a twist of lemon juice, some soy sauce and mirin and you have something pretty special without too much effort.

And don't forget the humble potato cooked in its own skin. Large potatoes are best left unpeeled, wrapped in foil and cooked on the barbecue until the flesh inside is pillow soft, ready to be cut open and filled with butter, sour cream or labneh, and finished off with a sprinkling of salt and some soft herbs like parsley, chervil, tarragon or chives.

There is something magically atmospheric about the hiss of food on the barbecue and the irresistible aromas that accompany it. This is quick, simple cooking at its sizzling best.

Take the famous Jemaa el-Fna market, held in a large, medieval square in Marrakesh. By day it is a thriving maze of market goods, selling everything from orange juice to leather backpacks, with snake charmers, charlatans and magicians vying for attention. At night it transforms, in my mind, into the world's largest barbecue. Hundreds of food stalls are lit up by blurred fairy lights, made

FIRED UP VEGETARIAN

even more romantic by the thick shroud of barbecue smoke in the air. So special is this place that it has been proclaimed a UNESCO Masterpiece of the Oral and Intangible Heritage of Humanity.

The Aw Taw Kaw market in Bangkok is similarly famous for its smoking woks and hotplates, sizzling with barbecued treats. Here, the metal skewers of the Middle Eastern kebab give way to bamboo skewers, and I have included plenty of recipes for both styles of kebab in this book.

Tender vine vegetables such as small heirloom tomatoes, zucchini (courgette) and eggplant (aubergine) are naturally skewerable. You can skewer just about any vegetable you like, although do remember to partly cook harder root vegetables beforehand, to give them a chance to cook through. Skewered vegies like big flavours, so alternate them with cubes of firm cheese such as haloumi or Indian paneer. Cook until the cheese is golden and the vegies tender, then finish off with some herbs and a tangy citrus-based dressing.

I use my new barbecue as an oven of sorts. Most modern barbecues have lids and mine, with its stainless steel encasing, conducts and radiates heat really well. When cooking breads, and for nicely charred vegies and cheese, preheat the grill and hotplate burners to high and close the lid. You will see the thermometer rise and the barbecue will then act like an oven. You can sit a cooking rack on the hotplate or grill, keeping food off the direct heat, to make the most perfect and authentic breads; in particular it's a great way to cook pocket bread. (The lid of the barbecue, by the way, is also a great spot to prove bread dough.) But don't stress if your barbecue doesn't have a lid — an upturned metal mixing bowl will do the same job.

And do use all those inventions of convenience in your kitchen as well. Cook saucy things in little heatproof pots directly on the barbecue. Tear off a sheet of baking paper to cook the food on, especially soft ingredients like tomatoes and cheese — your food will still have appetising grill marks, but without the mess, and the corners of the paper can be used to pick up the cooked food and tumble it into a bowl or straight onto a platter. Wrap food in foil or baking paper to make parcels that are steamed within; for an air of added drama, these barbecued parcels can be served and unwrapped at the table.

Choose quality, seasonally fresh ingredients, stick to the classic flavour combinations, introduce a variation or two to keep things interesting and you can't go wrong. If you are even remotely familiar with vegetarian cooking, you'll know this already. And if not, after tasting some of the recipes in this book, you'll hopefully agree that vegetarian cookery definitely deserves a place on the barbecue.

9

TYPES OF BARBECUES

Compared to other foods, cooking vegetarian recipes on the barbecue involves relatively little mess and little smoke, which offers greater flexibility. Still, when testing the recipes in my barbecue books, I usually do so on my old front verandah, so I can make as much mess and smoke as I need to.

I often find myself developing recipes in winter, and because of deadlines I can't always wait for the sun to shine before I start barbecuing. The great thing about the vegetarian recipes in this book is that in wet or cold weather you can simply cook them inside on an electric grill or hotplate! But this is really defeating the social nature of barbecuing, so I'm assuming for this book that you will generally be cooking outdoors.

Here are the main pros and cons for the different contraptions you can use.

ELECTRIC

Electric barbecues offer a mobile and convenient way of cooking, and are ideal for apartment living. Even better if you have a balcony, so you feel like you are barbecuing outdoors. But they do have downsides: electric barbecues and grills often have a built-in thermostat that cuts out the heat, meaning you have less control when cooking. Not ideal when barbecuing.

GAS

Cooking with gas gives you excellent control over the heat, which is what a good barbecue is all about. However, with a gas barbecue, you can never cook using LPG indoors; the other issue is making sure you actually have gas to burn, and

topping up the LPG tank is not always convenient or inexpensive. Some outdoor barbecues have the luxury of town or natural gas piped directly into them.

WOOD

Wood barbecues require attention, but are fun to use and produce a barbecued result like no other. Maintaining the heat is tricky and it will take time to master a wood-fired barbecue. They are ideal in the great outdoors and in a big backyard. But because they are generally constructed of brick, they aren't at all mobile, which is an obvious limitation.

COAL

Coal barbecues are designed as compact, mobile units, which equates to convenience. They range in size and function, with many of the larger charcoal barbecues designed to slow-cook big cuts of meat. Like gas barbecues, they obviously cannot be used indoors, but are great if you have a backyard or even a small balcony.

In Japan, what we know as a hibachi was actually designed to heat homes, not to cook with. In America the hibachi grill has become synonymous with quick, efficient and healthy grilling.

Smaller coal barbecues can actually be placed in the centre of the table, making the barbecue experience very interactive.

DIPS & BITS

What often makes a barbecue memorable are all those extra things. The things we often see and taste first, all ready to go, set up at the table. Some we try to forget, like a tub of sour cream mixed up with dehydrated French onion soup and given the title 'French onion dip'. Remember that beauty? While this is not what I call cooking, it is the stuff of memories.

And how often do you hear 'that was the best dip', 'what was in that sauce?' or 'I must have the recipe for that dressing!'?

It doesn't really matter what it is, it comes back to the same thing: the experience that is sharing. I have found that if the scene is set for a lovely, relaxed day, or night, the enjoyment of the food is enhanced. I wonder if this explains our love of a barbecue. Or when we say the very word 'barbecue' we think a sunny day, party, celebration, fun.

Most of the recipes here make use of the barbecue. Except for a few salad dressings, I think it is essential that the barbecue be used at some stage of the recipe. If you have the space, the time and the weather permits, why not make the whole thing barbecue-side? Peel and mash the sweet pumpkin, sprinkle a mixture of Arabian spices over just-hot flatbread, swirl golden corn through sour cream, or have a guest stir the fresh salsa ingredients together.

PUMPKIN, BLACK BEAN & FETA DIP

Serves 8–10

1 butternut pumpkin (squash), about 1.5 kg (3 lb 5 oz)
2 tablespoons olive oil
1 teaspoon ground cumin
½ teaspoon cayenne pepper
400 g (14 oz) tinned black beans, rinsed and well drained
100 g (3½ oz) feta cheese, crumbled
½ cup chopped coriander (cilantro) leaves and stalks
½ teaspoon sea salt
extra virgin olive oil, for drizzling
chargrilled bread, to serve

This dip is a cinch. You take one really nice-looking pumpkin and cook it on the grill until the skin is blackened — for about an hour, give or take. There is no strict timing here, it depends on the size and shape of the pumpkin. The inspiration came from my Barbie Ghanoush recipe, where the eggplant (aubergine) is kept whole and simply cooked on a grill. That recipe is on page 25. Check it out.

Preheat the barbecue grill to medium.

Sit the pumpkin on the grill and close the lid, if you have one, or cover with a metal bowl. Cook for about an hour, turning often until the skin of the pumpkin is blackened all over. Remove the pumpkin from the grill and allow to cool slightly.

When cool enough to handle, peel the tough skin off the pumpkin and discard it. Cut the pumpkin lengthways down the middle and scoop out the seeds.

Roughly chop the flesh of the pumpkin and place in a large bowl. Add the olive oil, cumin, cayenne pepper, beans, feta, coriander and salt and use a fork to combine. Drizzle with extra virgin olive oil and serve with chargrilled bread.

NOTE: This dip will keep in an airtight container in the fridge for 2–3 days.

14

FIRED UP VEGETARIAN

CHIMICHURRI

Chimichurri is an Argentinian salsa verde or, simply put, green sauce. But this herbaceous green sauce is more rugged than its European counterparts. Some say chimichurri should taste like it has been dragged through the herb garden, and that's a pretty good description.

Preheat the barbecue grill to high.

Place the tomato, spring onions and garlic on the grill. Use metal tongs to turn the vegies until the skins are charred — almost blackened — all over. Remove from the heat and allow to cool.

When cool enough to handle, peel the vegies and garlic and discard the charred skins. Don't be too fussy about removing all the skins — they'll add a smoky flavour to the chimichurri.

Place all the vegies and the garlic in a food processor and blitz until finely chopped. Add the herbs, oregano and salt and pulse to combine.

With the motor running, add the oil, then the vinegar, to make a smooth sauce.

Serve with chargrilled potato wedges as a dip, or spoon over chargrilled eggplant (aubergine).

NOTES: The chimichurri will keep in an airtight container in the fridge for 2–3 days.

For this recipe I prefer to use Greek oregano, sold in bunches with the leaves and stems still intact. It is sweeter and somehow less medicinal tasting than the pre-packaged stuff.

To chargrill potato wedges, first parboil them until nearly tender, then drain well and allow to cool completely on a tray. Chargrill them on a hot barbecue grill for a few minutes on each side before serving.

1 large, ripe tomato
4 spring onions (scallions)
4 garlic cloves, unpeeled
6 cups roughly chopped flat-leaf (Italian) parsley
2 cups chopped coriander (cilantro) leaves and stalks
½ teaspoon dried Greek oregano (see Notes)
½ teaspoon sea salt
60 ml (2 fl oz/¼ cup) olive oil
60 ml (2 fl oz/¼ cup) white wine vinegar
chargrilled potato wedges, to serve (see Notes)

SMOKY TOMATO, GARLIC & LIME SALSA

Serves 4–6

4 vine-ripened tomatoes
2 large green chillies,
    finely sliced
2 garlic cloves, roughly chopped
2 tablespoons lime juice
½ teaspoon sea salt
1 teaspoon caster (superfine)
    sugar
30 g (1 oz/½ cup) thinly sliced
    spring onions (scallions)
1 cup roughly chopped coriander
    (cilantro) leaves and stalks
organic corn chips, to serve

Thai food was one of my first cuisine crushes, and this recipe is one of the oldest in my repertoire. The Thai version of this salsa would include fish sauce and lime juice. You can just imagine how good that would be, too.

Preheat the barbecue grill and hotplate to high.

Put the tomatoes on the grill and cook, turning often, so the skin blisters and blackens. Remove from the heat and leave until cool enough to handle.

Cut out and discard the core of each tomato. Cut the tomatoes in half and gently squeeze out some of the liquid and seeds.

Put the tomatoes, including any bits of burnt skin, in a food processor with the chilli and garlic. Blitz until finely chopped, then spoon into a bowl. Stir in the lime juice, salt, sugar, spring onion and coriander. Check the taste and add more salt if needed.

Loosely wrap the corn chips in foil. Sit the foil parcel on the barbecue hotplate for a couple of minutes to heat through.

Serve the dip with the warm corn chips on the side.

FIRED UP VEGETARIAN

ARABIAN SPICE MIX

Makes about ½ cup

This is my simplified version of za'atar, a Middle Eastern spice blend. Okay, so the spice mix isn't actually cooked on the barbecue, but it's such a fabulous accompaniment to barbecued foods that I just had to include it. It's particularly delicious sprinkled over chargrilled bread and sliced vine-ripened tomatoes.

2 tablespoons sesame seeds
2 tablespoons dried thyme
2 tablespoons sumac (see Notes)
1 teaspoon sea salt
grilled flatbreads, to serve
extra virgin olive oil, to serve

Put the sesame seeds in a small dry frying pan over medium heat. Cook, shaking the pan regularly, until evenly golden. Tip into a bowl and allow to cool.

Put the sesame seeds, thyme, sumac and salt in a spice mill and process into a rough powder, or grind to a rough powder using a mortar and pestle.

Serve sprinkled on grilled flatbreads dipped in olive oil.

NOTES: Store any unused spice mix in an airtight container in a cool, dark place. It will keep for several months, but is best used within a few weeks for maximum flavour.

Sumac is a spice ground from a purple berry, widely used in Middle Eastern cuisine. It has a pleasantly astringent lemony flavour and is available from specialty grocers and spice shops.

GREEN TOMATO & CAPERBERRY SALSA

Serves 6–8

4 green tomatoes, cores removed, flesh finely diced
80 g (2¾ oz/½ cup) caperberries, chopped
1 red onion, finely diced
60 ml (2 fl oz/¼ cup) white vinegar
½ teaspoon sea salt
½ teaspoon caster (superfine) sugar
½ cup finely chopped coriander (cilantro) leaves and stalks
½ cup finely chopped mint
grilled haloumi, to serve

This salsa, or sauce, is great spooned over barbecued haloumi, tofu or firm mozzarella cheese. Try tumbling corn chips onto a serving plate and simply topping them with this salsa and some light sour cream. Very nice.

Combine all the ingredients in a serving bowl. Cover and set aside for 30 minutes for the flavours to develop.

Serve at room temperature.

NOTE: The salsa will keep in an airtight container in the fridge for 2–3 days.

20

JALAPEÑO JAM

Serves 8–10

If chilli is your thing, this jam is for you. Spread it over chargrilled bread and spoon over some cottage cheese to cool the heat, or smear it over grilled corn cobs and squeeze some lime juice over to tang it all up a bit. Try sandwiching a layer of the jam and some grated feta cheese between two soft burritos and cook on the barbecue hotplate until golden and crisp. Or just keep it in the fridge and put it on anything you like.

500 g (1 lb 2 oz) green chillies (about 24)
2 garlic cloves
270 g (9½ oz) jar sliced jalapeño chillies, in vinegar
½ teaspoon sea salt
220 g (7¾ oz/1 cup) sugar
chargrilled bread, to serve
chargrilled vegetables, to serve

Preheat the barbecue grill and hotplate to high.

Leave the ends of the chillies intact and scatter the chillies over the hotplate and grill. Cook for 10–15 minutes, using metal tongs to frequently turn the chillies, removing them from the barbecue as they start to blister and char.

When cool enough to handle, peel off as much of the charred skin as possible. (Leaving some burnt bits is fine as they will add to the final flavour of the jam.)

Pull off and discard the chilli stems. Roughly chop the chillies, then place in a food processor with the garlic. Add the whole jar of jalapeños, including the liquid, and blitz until finely chopped.

Tip the paste into a saucepan and stir in the salt and sugar. Bring to the boil, then reduce the heat to a low simmer and cook for 30 minutes, stirring occasionally, until the mixture is thick and sticky-looking. You can test if the jam is ready by placing a spoonful on a cold plate. Run your finger through the middle of the jam — if the mixture stays where it is, the jam is ready.

Serve with chargrilled bread and vegetables.

NOTE: The jam will keep in an airtight container in the fridge for up to 10 days.

23

DIPS & BITS

MUHAMMARA

Serves 6-8

3 large red capsicums (peppers)
35 g (1¼ oz/¼ cup) walnuts
1 teaspoon ground cumin
½ teaspoon cayenne pepper
2 tablespoons pomegranate
  molasses
2 tablespoons lemon juice

There are many versions of this dip in Syria, although the combination of roasted red capsicums, walnuts and pomegranate molasses can be found in other parts of the Middle East, especially Turkey and Lebanon. Traditionally this dip contains breadcrumbs. I have not included them here, so this version is coeliac friendly.

Preheat the barbecue grill to high.

Cook the capsicums on the barbecue grill for 10–15 minutes, turning often, until the skins are blistered and blackened all over. Remove from the barbecue and allow to cool.

When cool enough to handle, peel and discard the skins. Cut the capsicums in half, then scoop out and discard the seeds.

Roughly chop the capsicum flesh and place in a food processor with the remaining ingredients. Process to a smooth, thick mixture.

Spoon into a serving dish and serve.

NOTE: This dip will keep in an airtight container in the fridge for about 1 week.

BARBIE GHANOUSH

This one is made for the barbecue. Actually, I don't believe you can achieve the same flavour without cooking the eggplant over a naked flame. The smokiness of the charred skin somehow gets into the flesh of the eggplant with really very little cooking time.

2 large eggplants (aubergines)
2 teaspoons sea salt
60 ml (2 fl oz/¼ cup) lemon juice
3 garlic cloves, crushed
2 tablespoons extra virgin olive
   oil, plus extra for drizzling
chargrilled Middle Eastern
   flatbread, to serve

Preheat the barbecue grill to high.

Prick each eggplant several times with a fork. Cook them on the barbecue grill for 10–15 minutes, turning often, until collapsed and tender. Remove from the barbecue and allow to cool on a tray.

When cool enough to handle, strip off and discard the skin of each eggplant. Place the flesh in a sieve over a bowl and set aside for 15 minutes to drain.

Put the eggplant flesh in a food processor with the salt, lemon juice, garlic and olive oil. Whiz to a purée, then pour the mixture into a bowl and drizzle with a little more olive oil.

Serve at room temperature, with chargrilled flatbread.

NOTE: The barbie ghanoush will keep in an airtight container in the fridge for 2–3 days.

DIPS & BITS

SPANISH DRESSING

Makes 225 ml (7½ fl oz)

125 ml (4 fl oz/½ cup) Spanish
    extra virgin olive oil
2 tablespoons sherry vinegar
2 tablespoons lemon juice
½ teaspoon sea salt

I use this dressing to toss through salads, douse over grilled cheese and to dunk bread in.

Place all the ingredients in a jar, seal the lid tightly and shake well. Store in the fridge for up to 2 weeks; shake well before using.

ROASTED GARLIC CRÈME

Serves 6–8

2 garlic bulbs, left whole
    and unpeeled
½ teaspoon sea salt
250 ml (9 fl oz/1 cup) rice bran oil
2 egg yolks, at room temperature
1 teaspoon mustard powder
2 tablespoons lemon juice

Similar to an aïoli, this luscious mayo is fabulous with grilled vegetables, especially root vegies.

Preheat the barbecue hotplate to medium.

Cut each garlic bulb in half horizontally through the middle. Sit each garlic half, cut side up, on a small sheet of foil. Sprinkle with the salt and drizzle with some of the oil. Loosely wrap each garlic half in the foil and sit them on the hotplate. Cook for 30 minutes, turning often with tongs, until the garlic is very soft.

Remove from the heat and allow the garlic to cool in the foil. Squeeze the softened garlic flesh out of the skins, directly into the bowl of a food processor, discarding the skins. Add the egg yolks, mustard powder and lemon juice and pulse to combine.

With the motor running, gradually add the remaining oil in a thin, steady stream and process until the mixture is emulsified and looks like thick custard. Add about 60 ml (2 fl oz/¼ cup) warm water and blend until smooth and creamy.

Serve warm, or cover and keep in the fridge for up to 3 days.

28

FIRED UP VEGETARIAN

NO FRILLS HOLLANDAISE

Makes about 250 ml (9 fl oz/1 cup)

No frills because you don't need a double boiler, and no frills because it saves on washing up. Dip in some potato wedges, hot off the grill.

2 egg yolks, at room temperature
½ teaspoon sea salt
60 ml (2 fl oz/¼ cup) rice bran oil
125 g (4½ oz) unsalted butter
2 tablespoons tarragon vinegar

Put the egg yolks and salt in a food processor and whiz to combine. With the motor running, slowly add the oil in a thin, steady stream and process until the mixture thickens slightly.

Put the butter in a small saucepan and cook over medium heat until bubbling hot, but not burnt. Pour the butter into a jug.

With the motor running, slowly pour the hot butter into the egg mixture. Add the vinegar and process until the mixture resembles custard.

Serve the hollandaise warm, or pour into an airtight container and keep in the fridge for up to 3 days.

TZATZIKI

Serves 8

This dip is best enjoyed as soon as it is made. It's great with falafel — either dip the falafel straight in, or smear the tzatziki over flatbread before wrapping up some lightly mashed falafel, fresh tomato and crisp lettuce.

390 g (13¾ oz/1½ cups)
    Greek-style yoghurt
2 garlic cloves, crushed
1 teaspoon ground cumin
½ teaspoon sea salt
1 Lebanese (short) cucumber,
    coarsely grated

Combine the yoghurt, garlic, cumin and salt in a bowl. Stir the cucumber through just before serving.

29

DIPS & BITS

GRILLED SWEETCORN & SOUR CREAM DIP

Serves 6-8

4 whole fresh corn cobs,
    preferably unpeeled
1 tablespoon rice bran oil
2 teaspoons dijon mustard
1 red onion, sliced into thick rings
½ cup finely chopped coriander
    (cilantro) leaves and stalks,
    plus extra leaves to garnish
3 tablespoons chopped flat-leaf
    (Italian) parsley
1 tablespoon white wine vinegar
½ teaspoon hot pepper sauce,
    plus extra for drizzling
1 teaspoon sea salt
370 g (12¾ oz/1½ cups)
    sour cream
warm flatbread, to serve

I have a café in the grounds of an art gallery. We made this dip to be photographed and afterwards I served it up to the staff at the gallery. Wow, what a positive response this one received. I served the dip with a crusty baked baguette and it was devoured in no time.

Preheat the barbecue grill to high.

Peel the corn and discard the husks. Brush the corn with the oil and the mustard. Brush the onion rings on both sides with the oil. Grill the corn and onion for 10–12 minutes, or until golden, turning often. Remove from the barbecue and allow to cool.

Cut the kernels from the cobs and place in a food processor. Roughly chop the onions and add them with the coriander, parsley, vinegar, pepper sauce and salt. Whiz until well combined but not too finely chopped — you want some texture in the dip.

Just before serving, combine the corn mixture and the sour cream in a bowl. Drizzle with extra pepper sauce, garnish with extra coriander and serve with warm flatbread.

30

**FIRED UP
VEGETARIAN**

SMALL PLATES

This is sociable food. This is tasty food, packed with lots of flavour. And that is the key to any cocktail food, finger food or plattered food. The barbecue can be used to entertain on any level.

Whatever you call it, this is flavourful food enjoyed in a few quick bites, leaving you wanting more. So, for maximum taste I use lots of seasoning in the form of spices. Fragrant and aromatic spices that excite the palate. And let's not forget lots of citrus, chilli and herbs.

You may not think that 'cheese' and 'barbecue' go together. But some cheeses are made to grill — like the salty, hard haloumi, smoked mozzarella, Indian paneer or Maltese gbejna. And these cheeses hold their own with strong flavours. They can be cubed and skewered, or bundled up in vine leaves.

The following small plates are a good way to start the occasion. Serve up several choices and pass them around for a very social barbecue.

GRILLED LOTUS WITH SPICED JAPANESE SALT

Serves 4

300 g (10½ oz) fresh lotus root, peeled and cut into thin slices
2 tablespoons tamari (Japanese soy sauce)
1 teaspoon sesame oil
lemon wedges, to serve

SPICED JAPANESE SALT
½ teaspoon white sesame seeds
½ teaspoon black sesame seeds
2 teaspoons sea salt
¼ teaspoon cayenne pepper
2 tablespoons finely chopped nori (dried seaweed)

I would not expect you to find fresh lotus root. Although, if you do, please use it. Frozen lotus root is sold in Asian supermarkets and is easier to slice than fresh lotus root, and for best results in this recipe, it does need to be sliced thinly. If you are new to the flavour of lotus root, I can best describe it as nutty and savoury — very nicely complemented by the spiced Japanese salt.

Put the lotus slices in a flat dish with the soy sauce and sesame oil and turn to coat. Cover and refrigerate for 3–6 hours, turning often.

To make the spiced Japanese salt, put all the sesame seeds and the salt in a small frying pan. Cook over high heat, shaking the pan, until the mixture just starts to smoke and the white sesame seeds and salt begin to lightly colour — be careful not to burn the seeds or they will become bitter.

Remove from the heat and allow to cool. Stir in the cayenne pepper and nori and transfer to an airtight container.

Preheat the barbecue grill to high.

Cook the lotus for 2–3 minutes on each side, or until golden.

Serve sprinkled with the spiced salt, with lemon wedges on the side for squeezing over.

NOTE: Any unused spiced salt will keep in an airtight jar in a cool, dark place for up to 1 month. It is also delicious as a seasoning sprinkled over plain boiled rice, tofu, boiled eggs and avocado.

34

FIRED UP VEGETARIAN

GRILLED CORN WITH JALAPEÑO, LIME & PARMESAN BUTTER

Serves 4

This recipe could easily be in the 'Sides & Salads' chapter. But whenever I have eaten this I haven't wanted to share it, so it subsequently became my very own small plate.

It might sound odd, but the parmesan really does work a treat with the bite and tang of the other ingredients. It actually complements them. Because there are so few ingredients here, quality is the key: good butter, good cheese.

Put all the ingredients for the jalapeño, lime and parmesan butter in a food processor and whiz until smooth. Scrape into a bowl, then cover and refrigerate until needed.

Preheat the barbecue grill to high. Cut the jalapeño, lime and parmesan butter into small pieces and leave at room temperature.

Cook the corn on the hotplate for 10–12 minutes, turning often, until the kernels are dark and caramelised.

Using metal tongs, put the hot corn cobs in a bowl. Add the butter and toss the corn around so it melts the butter.

Tumble the corn cobs onto a serving plate and pour over any melted butter remaining in the bowl. Garnish with coriander and serve with lime cheeks.

NOTE: You can make the jalapeño, lime and parmesan butter up to a week ahead, or wrap it thoroughly and freeze for up to 1 month.

4 corn cobs, each cut into
    3 smaller rounds
coriander (cilantro) sprigs,
    to garnish
lime cheeks, to serve

JALAPEÑO, LIME &
PARMESAN BUTTER
125 g (4½ oz) unsalted
    butter, softened to
    room temperature
2 tablespoons pickled jalapeño
    chillies, well drained and
    chopped
1 tablespoon lime juice
25 g (1 oz/¼ cup) finely
    grated parmesan cheese

BLACKENED PANEER SKEWERS

Serves 4

400 g (14 oz) block paneer
lemon wedges, to serve

BLACKENED SEASONING
60 ml (2 fl oz/¼ cup) rice bran oil
2 teaspoons dried thyme
2 teaspoons dried oregano
2 teaspoons hot smoked
   Spanish paprika
1 teaspoon cayenne pepper
1 teaspoon sea salt

FRESH TOMATO RELISH
2 roma (plum) tomatoes,
   finely diced
1 small red onion, finely diced
2 teaspoons soft brown sugar
2 tablespoons lime juice
½ teaspoon celery seeds
¼ teaspoon nigella seeds
   (see Note)

Paneer is an Indian 'cheese', though not what Westerners would call cheese. It is a fresh cheese and does not use a setting agent. Have you ever left fresh ricotta in the fridge for several days? It becomes very firm, just like paneer — which, by the way, is so good in curries too.

Combine the blackened seasoning ingredients in a bowl, then pour the mixture onto a flat plate.

Cut the paneer into eight rectangles, about 1.5 cm (⅝ inch) wide and 6 cm (2½ inches) long — like fat chips. Roll each piece in the blackened seasoning mixture to coat all over. Cover and marinate in the refrigerator for several hours.

Soak eight bamboo skewers in cold water for 30 minutes.

Meanwhile, combine all the tomato relish ingredients in a bowl and set aside for the flavours to develop.

Preheat the barbecue grill to high. Thread a bamboo skewer through each piece of paneer. Cook the skewers, turning every couple of minutes, for 8–10 minutes, or until dark and aromatic. Serve immediately, with the tomato relish and lemon wedges.

NOTE: Nigella seeds look like little black sesame seeds, but have a peppery, smoky flavour. They are widely used throughout India, Egypt and the Middle East. You'll find them in spice shops and gourmet food stores.

38

**FIRED UP
VEGETARIAN**

GRILLED MOZZARELLA WITH TOMATO, HONEY & CINNAMON JAM

Serves 4

Imagine this... I go to an Italian restaurant in the middle of nowhere, run by women from Rome. A starter dish of simply grilled smoked mozzarella (but, just quietly, the cheese works just as well unsmoked) appears. It is utterly delicious. This is my version, barbecue style.

Cut the mozzarella into eight slices, about 1 cm (½ inch) thick. Keep the cheese cold in the fridge until you are ready to cook it.

To make the jam, heat the oil in a small saucepan over high heat. Add the onion and cook for 2–3 minutes, or until softened and starting to turn golden. Add the sugar and stir for a minute or so. The sugar will crystallise and the onion will deepen in colour.

Carefully add the tomato — it will bubble on contact with the hot sugar. Stir in the cinnamon, reduce the heat to medium and simmer for 5 minutes, stirring often, until the tomato deepens in colour. Stir in the honey and cook for a further 10 minutes, stirring often so the mixture doesn't stick to the pan.

Preheat the barbecue grill or hotplate to high and lightly brush with oil. Lay the mozzarella slices on the hotplate and cook for 1 minute, or until the edges just start to melt. Quickly turn the slices over and cook for another minute.

Serve hot, with a good dollop of jam and a sprinkling of parsley.

NOTE: Choose the firmest brand of mozzarella available. Fresh mozzarella cannot be cooked this way.

You can also serve each slice of mozzarella on a treviso or radicchio leaf and sprinkle the dolloped jam with sesame seeds.

500 g (1 lb 2 oz) smoked
    mozzarella (see Note)
rice bran oil, for brushing
finely chopped parsley,
    to garnish

TOMATO, HONEY &
CINNAMON JAM
1 tablespoon rice bran oil
1 small red onion, cut in half
    lengthways, then cut into
    thin wedges
1 tablespoon caster (superfine)
    sugar
400 g (14 oz) tin chopped tomatoes
½ teaspoon ground cinnamon
2 tablespoons honey

HALOUMI, MINT & PRESERVED LEMON CIGARS

Serves 4–6

6 filo pastry sheets, each
    measuring 44 x 28 cm
    (17½ x 11¼ inches)
200 g (7 oz) block haloumi
    cheese
2 tablespoons finely chopped
    mint leaves
2 tablespoons olive oil
12 thin strips of preserved
    lemon rind
sea salt, for sprinkling
lemon wedges, to serve

I love filo pastry. I use it to top, to wrap, to stuff and to roll, savoury or sweet. It's cheap, and you might be surprised to learn that it cooks very well on a hotplate. Enter barbecue. Need I say more.

Lay the filo sheets on top of each other. Cut the stack in half lengthways, then cut across in half to give 24 smaller rectangles of pastry. Lay the rectangles on top of each other and cover with a damp cloth.

Cut the haloumi into 12 thin fingers. Combine the mint and olive oil in a bowl.

Lay two filo rectangles on top of each other and brush with some of the oil from the bowl. Put a piece of haloumi on the short end of the pastry, top with a strip of preserved lemon, then fold the sides of the filo over the haloumi and roll up into a cigar shape. Repeat to make 12 cigars.

Preheat the barbecue hotplate to medium.

Cook the cigars on the hotplate for 4–5 minutes, turning often, until the pastry is golden and charred. Sprinkle with a little sea salt and serve hot, with lemon wedges on the side.

CHICKPEA & PUMPKIN PAKORA

Serves 4–6

///

Best put, a pakora is a fried snack — although we are barbecuing them, not frying them here. These fritters are delicious, made even more so by their simplicity.

Bring a large saucepan of water to the boil. Add the chickpeas and pumpkin and cook for 15 minutes, or until the pumpkin is tender. Drain well, then tip the chickpeas and pumpkin into a bowl.

Use a potato masher to mash the chickpeas and pumpkin into a lumpy mixture. Sir in the peas, chilli, spring onion, chickpea flour, cumin, ground coriander, fresh coriander, lemon juice and salt. Cover and refrigerate until chilled.

Divide the mixture into eight even portions. Using wet hands, form the portions into discs or patties. Place on a tray lined with baking paper and refrigerate until ready to cook.

Preheat the barbecue hotplate to medium–high and brush with oil. Lightly dust the the fritters with extra chickpea flour and place them on the hotplate. Cook for 3–4 minutes on each side, or until golden.

Serve warm, garnished with coriander leaves, with lettuce, lemon wedges and yoghurt on the side.

NOTE: These fritters can be made a day in advance. Cover with plastic wrap and refrigerate until you're ready to cook them.

300 g (10½ oz) tinned chickpeas, drained
500 g (1 lb 2 oz) piece of jap pumpkin, peeled, seeded and roughly chopped, to yield about 300 g (10½ oz) flesh
140 g (5 oz/1 cup) frozen peas
1 large green chilli, thinly sliced on an angle
2 spring onions (scallions), thinly sliced on an angle
60 g (2¼ oz/½ cup) chickpea flour (besan), plus extra for dusting
1 teaspoon cumin seeds
1 teaspoon ground coriander
3 tablespoons finely chopped coriander (cilantro) leaves and stalks, plus extra leaves to garnish
1 tablespoon lemon juice
½ teaspoon sea salt
rice bran oil, for brushing
iceberg lettuce leaves, to serve
lemon wedges, to serve
plain yoghurt, to serve

EXOTIC EGGPLANT SKEWERS WITH THAI HERB SALAD

Serves 8

12 round Thai green eggplants
   (aubergines)
60 ml (2 fl oz/¼ cup) kecap manis
1 tablespoon rice bran oil

THAI HERB SALAD
2 cups roughly chopped
   coriander (cilantro) leaves
   and stalks
2 cups Thai basil leaves
2 cups mint leaves
55 g (2 oz/½ cup) finely sliced
   red Asian shallots
2 long red chillies, finely sliced
   on an angle

DRESSING
1 tablespoon Maggi seasoning
1 tablespoon lemon juice
2 teaspoons sesame oil
1 teaspoon caster (superfine)
   sugar

I am a fan of the Thai eggplant (aubergine) varieties. The small pea or round apple eggplants have a crunchy bitterness that works well on the barbecue. But if they're not your thing, use your favourite eggplant instead, cut into large chunks. It will work just as nicely.

Cut each eggplant in half. Place in a bowl with the kecap manis and oil, tossing to coat well. Cover and set aside for 3 hours for the flavours to penetrate.

Soak eight long bamboo skewers in cold water for 30 minutes.

Meanwhile, combine the Thai herb salad ingredients in a bowl and set aside. Combine the dressing ingredients in a small bowl, stir to dissolve the sugar, then set aside also.

Preheat the barbecue grill to high.

Thread the eggplant onto the skewers. Place on the grill and cook, turning often, for 8–10 minutes, or until the eggplant is very tender. Arrange the skewers and salad on a serving platter.

Stir the dressing again, drizzle it over the salad and eggplant and serve.

46

**FIRED UP
VEGETARIAN**

INDIAN BREAD WITH TRUCK-STOP POTATOES

Serves 6–8

2 large boiling potatoes, such as desiree (about 600 g/1 lb 5 oz), cut into quarters
1 teaspoon sea salt
½ teaspoon dried mango powder (see Note)
½ teaspoon chilli powder
1 teaspoon toasted cumin seeds
1 teaspoon garam masala
1 cup finely chopped coriander (cilantro) leaves and stalks
1 large green chilli, finely chopped
8 ready-made, yeast-free naan roti
Indian fruit chutney or pickle, to serve

In India, local roadside restaurants, usually located at highway truck-stops, are called dhabas. I guess the equivalent in the West would be roadside cafes. Give me the food in a dhaba any time, which is typically home-made and heavily spiced — just how I like it. The bread in a dhaba would be yeasted and stuffed with the potatoes.

I have adapted this recipe to use ready-made, yeast-free flatbread. Quick, easy and extremely tasty.

Peel the potatoes and place in a saucepan. Add enough cold water to just cover them and place over high heat. When the water boils, cover the pan and turn the heat off. Leave for 20 minutes, or until the potatoes are tender but not falling apart. (This is also a great way to cook potatoes for a potato salad — they always have the perfect firmness!)

Drain the potatoes and allow to cool to room temperature. When cool enough to handle, coarsely grate the potatoes into a bowl. Add the salt, spices, coriander and chilli and stir until just combined.

Preheat the barbecue hotplate to medium.

Spread half the potato mixture over a piece of roti and lay another on top. Press down gently to join the two together. Repeat to make another three potato breads.

Cook the breads on the hotplate until just golden on both sides. Cut into thick wedges and serve warm, with your favourite Indian chutney or pickle.

NOTE: Also called amchur or amchoor, dried mango powder is made from ground dried green mangoes and is used in northern Indian cookery to add a tangy, sour fruit flavour to dishes. You'll find it in Indian grocery stores and good spice shops.

48

SMOKED TOFU, CHILLI & VEGETABLE CABBAGE ROLLS

Serves 4

Cabbage leaves are used in so many cuisines, especially throughout Asia. And anything rolled in them is good — it means you can make them in advance, refrigerate them, then cook them up at a minute's notice.

Bring a large saucepan of water to the boil. Add the cabbage leaves, turn the heat off and set aside for 2 minutes — the leaves will be tender but bright green.

Drain well and rinse under cold water until completely cool. Drain, then trim any thick ends off the cabbage leaves. Lay the leaves on a clean cloth on a work surface and leave to dry.

To make the filling, combine the tofu, sprouts, carrot, ginger, chilli and coriander in a bowl. Combine the tamari, sesame oil, vinegar, sugar and cornflour in another bowl, then pour the mixture over the vegetables. Season to taste with freshly ground black pepper and stir to combine.

To assemble, place about ½ cup of the filling on the broad end of one cabbage leaf. Fold the end over the filling, then fold the sides in, rolling to enclose the filling, and finishing at the stem of the leaf. Don't wrap too tightly, and don't worry if some of the filling sticks out the sides. Repeat with the remaining filling and leaves to make eight rolls.

Tear off eight pieces of foil, large enough to fully wrap up the cabbage rolls, and lay them on a flat surface. Brush the top of each piece of foil with oil. Roll each of the cabbage rolls up in a sheet of foil, twisting the ends to seal.

Preheat a barbecue hotplate to medium. Sit the cabbage rolls on the hotplate and cook for 10 minutes, turning every few minutes.

Serve the rolls on a platter, to be unwrapped at the table.

8 large Chinese cabbage
  (wong bok) leaves
grapeseed oil, for brushing

FILLING
100 g (3½ oz) smoked tofu,
  roughly grated
115 g (4 oz/1 cup) bean sprouts
155 g (5½ oz/1 cup) grated carrot
1 teaspoon finely grated fresh
  ginger
1 small red chilli, finely sliced
½ cup finely chopped coriander
  (cilantro) leaves and stalks
2 tablespoons tamari (Japanese
  soy sauce)
1 teaspoon sesame oil
1 tablespoon rice vinegar
½ teaspoon sugar
1 teaspoon cornflour
  (cornstarch)

49

SMALL PLATES

HALOUMI WITH PICKLED CHILLI & CAULIFLOWER SALSA

Serves 4

I am thinking I like the word salsa, which really means sauce: it evokes such a sense of freshness and simplicity of flavour. And here the star player is cauliflower, which is often overlooked, yet lends itself to all styles of cooking — baking, frying, boiling. Just serve it with something cheesy and it shines.

To make the salsa, heat the olive oil in large frying pan over high heat. Add the cauliflower and stir-fry for 4–5 minutes, or until golden and tender.

Stir the garlic and onion through and cook for just a minute, then remove from the heat and allow to cool.

Stir in the vinegar, chillies and herbs. Set aside while cooking the haloumi, to allow the flavours to develop.

Preheat the barbecue grill to high.

Brush the haloumi with the rice bran oil. Spread the slices on the grill and cook for 2–3 minutes on each side, or until golden grill marks appear.

Layer the haloumi and salsa on a serving plate. Serve warm.

400 g (14 oz) haloumi, cut into slices 5 mm (¼ inch) thick
1 tablespoon rice bran oil

PICKLED CHILLI & CAULIFLOWER SALSA
1 tablespoon light olive oil
250 g (9 oz/2 cups) small cauliflower florets
1 garlic clove, finely chopped
1 red onion, chopped
2 tablespoons sherry vinegar
60 g (2¼ oz/½ cup) finely sliced pickled red chillies
3 tablespoons finely shredded mint leaves
3 tablespoons finely chopped flat-leaf (Italian) parsley

51

SMALL PLATES

MALTESE CHEESE WITH OLIVE, PARSLEY & PRESERVED LEMON SALAD

Serves 6

12 large vine leaves in brine, drained
6 individual Maltese cheeses, about 80 g (2¾ oz) each
2 tablespoons olive oil

OLIVE, PARSLEY & PRESERVED LEMON SALAD
95 g (3¼ oz/½ cup) kalamata olives, pitted and chopped
1 cup roughly chopped flat-leaf (Italian) parsley
1 tablespoon finely chopped preserved lemon rind
2 spring onions (scallions), thinly sliced
1 garlic clove, crushed
60 ml (2 fl oz/¼ cup) olive oil
2 tablespoons lemon juice

At my local market, new ingredients come along every now and then and take my fancy. Gbejna, a cheese from Malta, is here to stay. It's not a precious cheese and it likes going with other strong flavours. You could instead use a firm ricotta, which will also hold its own with the lovely, intense flavours of olive and preserved lemon.

Soak the vine leaves in cold water for 30 minutes. Drain well and pat dry.

Lay two vine leaves on a work surface so they slightly overlap. Sit one of the cheeses on one end of the leaves. Drizzle with some of the olive oil, then wrap the cheese up in the vine leaves.

Repeat with the remaining vine leaves, cheese and oil to make six parcels.

Combine all the salad ingredients in a bowl. Set aside while grilling the cheese.

Preheat the barbecue grill to high. Sit the vine leaf parcels on the grill and cook, without turning, for 4–5 minutes, or until the cheese has heated through.

To serve, unwrap the cheeses and spoon the salad on top.

FIRED UP VEGETARIAN

CRISP VEGETABLE & HERB RICE PAPER ROLLS

Makes 12 rolls

I sometimes ask myself why it took me so long to realise the enjoyment of a rice paper roll. These are so yummy; fresh, fragrant and healthy. Well, they feel healthy. The rice paper itself is like thick cellophane, and is often served fresh after a brief soaking in cold water, rendering the sheets tender enough to fold around favoured ingredients. But the rolls can also be deep-fried, pan-fried, or even cooked on a barbecue!

Soak the noodles in warm water for 10 minutes, or until softened. Drain well in a colander. Use kitchen scissors to roughly chop the noodles into shorter lengths so they are easier to work with.

Combine the noodles in a bowl with the spring onion, herbs, garlic chives, carrots, bean sprouts and zucchini.

Combine the dipping sauce ingredients in a bowl and set aside.

Put some cold water in a flat dish that is wider than the rice paper rolls. Lay a clean cloth on a work surface.

Working one at a time, soak a rice paper sheet in the water for 2 minutes, until the rice paper is white and very soft. Lay the softened sheet flat on the cloth.

Take 3 tablespoons of the filling mixture and form a mound in the middle of the rice paper. Fold the sides over, then roll up to enclose the filling, to make a parcel. Repeat to make 12 rolls.

Preheat the barbecue hotplate to high and brush with a little rice bran oil. Sit the rolls on the hotplate and cook, turning often, for 4–5 minutes, or until golden all over.

Serve immediately, with the dipping sauce on the side.

NOTE: The dipping sauce can be made ahead and will keep for some days in the fridge in an airtight container.

50 g (1¾ oz) rice vermicelli noodles
125 g (4½ oz/1 cup) finely shredded spring onions (scallions)
1 cup chopped coriander (cilantro) leaves and stalks
1 cup chopped mint leaves
3 tablespoons finely chopped garlic chives
155 g (5½ oz/1 cup) grated carrot
115 g (4 oz/1 cup) bean sprouts
135 g (4¾ oz/1 cup) grated zucchini (courgette)
12 large round rice paper sheets, about 21 cm (8¼ inches) in diameter
rice bran oil, for brushing

DIPPING SAUCE
250 ml (9 fl oz/1 cup) hoisin sauce
60 ml (2 fl oz/¼ cup) orange juice
½ teaspoon sesame oil

KAFFIR LIME LEAF & LEMONGRASS TOFU

Serves 2

2 lemongrass stems, pale part
    only, chopped
2 garlic cloves, chopped
2 kaffir lime leaves, thinly sliced
1 tablespoon finely grated fresh
    ginger
1 tablespoon Maggi seasoning
2 tablespoons vegetable oil
1 teaspoon caster (superfine)
    sugar
300 g (10½ oz) block firm tofu
kecap manis, to serve
coriander (cilantro) sprigs,
    to garnish

I can totally understand if you don't enjoy tofu, as it is often cooked really badly. I mean, if you cooked a fillet steak for 20 minutes on each side you probably wouldn't like that either.

Tofu is about texture. It is a chameleon of sorts and takes on the flavours it is cooked with. So when cooked well — and by this I generally mean simply and quickly — and used with other flavours, you will understand why tofu is no longer only enjoyed by vegetarians.

If you can't get your hands on kecap manis, soy sauce with a little brown sugar will do the job nicely.

Put the lemongrass, garlic, lime leaves, ginger, seasoning, oil and sugar in a food processor and blend to make a chunky sauce.

Transfer the sauce to a bowl and add the tofu. Gently turn the tofu so it is evenly covered in the mixture. Cover and set aside at room temperature for a couple of hours.

Preheat the barbecue hotplate to medium. Lay a sheet of baking paper on the hotplate. Sit the tofu on the baking paper, scraping any sauce from the bowl over the tofu. Cook for 4–5 minutes.

Using a large metal spatula, turn the tofu over; the lemongrass mixture will have cooked golden and charred in some places. Cook for another 5 minutes.

Cut the tofu into thick slices or cubes and transfer to a serving plate. Drizzle with kecap manis, scatter with coriander and serve.

58

**FIRED UP
VEGETARIAN**

SOY & GINGER GRILLED MUSHROOMS

Serves 4

Try not to use really tiny mushrooms here — or for any barbecue cooking, for that matter. Little ones are a pain to barbecue. Big, steaky mushies, on the other hand, are easy to cook, have more flesh and are tastier.

Combine the wine, soy sauce, rice flour, sesame oil and ginger in a large bowl. Add the shiitake and Swiss brown mushrooms and toss to coat them in the marinade. Cover and set aside at room temperature for 3 hours, or refrigerate for 6 hours.

Preheat the barbecue hotplate to high. Pour the rice bran oil over the hotplate to grease it.

Remove the mushrooms from the marinade and tumble them onto the hotplate. Cook for 10–15 minutes, turning them often, until dark, tender and aromatic.

Add the oyster mushrooms and cook, turning, for 1–2 minutes, or until just tender. Serve hot, scattered with spring onion.

250 ml (9 fl oz/1 cup) red wine
250 ml (9 fl oz/1 cup) light
    soy sauce
2 tablespoons rice flour
1 tablespoon sesame oil
1 tablespoon finely grated
    fresh ginger
6 large shiitake mushrooms
6 large Swiss brown mushrooms
2 tablespoons rice bran oil
6 king oyster mushrooms,
    halved lengthways
100 g (3½ oz) oyster mushrooms
sliced spring onions (scallions),
    to serve

BIG PLATES

Many people assume that vegetarians are small eaters. Please don't. Especially so at a barbecue, where the vegetarian is often overlooked. And please don't let the vegetarian option be a tofu sausage or a frozen pattie. This is insulting to both the individual and to the many cuisines that have vegetarian cookery embedded in their culinary history.

Quite a few of the recipes in this chapter are simply my barbecued versions of some of the most delicious vegetarian dishes you can find: North African chakchouka, Chinese Buddha's delight, Japanese pancakes. Many of these dishes are in fact traditionally cooked on a barbecue, grill or hotplate. And with a little ingenuity, other dishes that weren't originally intended to be cooked on the barbecue can be given the grill treatment too. With a few tricks under your belt — such as wrapping food in lotus, vine or banana leaves, or using skewers — anything is possible.

There may well be times when your barbecue is about grazing, picking and dipping. But sometimes we want to eat like a man, or a woman. These recipes will fit the bill.

SILVERBEET & FETA GÖZLEME

Serves 4

1 tablespoon olive oil, plus
    extra for brushing
1 red onion, finely chopped
2 garlic cloves, crushed
180 g (6 oz) finely shredded
    silverbeet (Swiss chard)
200 g (7 oz) feta cheese, crumbled
50 g (1¾ oz/½ cup) coarsely
    grated cheddar cheese
¼ teaspoon sweet paprika
4 large Greek pitta breads, about
    26 cm (10½ inches) across
lemon wedges, to serve

Hot dog and doughnut stalls have been replaced by gözleme (Turkish pizza) stalls at markets. And this is not a bad thing. I love these 'pizzas'. It would be very tricky to try your hand at making the dough yourself, but you don't have to, not with so many exotic pre-made breads out there — including some good gluten-free ones too.

Combine the olive oil, onion, garlic, silverbeet, feta, cheddar and paprika in a bowl, mixing well.

Spread half the mixture over one pitta bread and top with another. Repeat with the remaining pitta breads and filling to make a second gözleme.

Preheat the barbecue hotplate to medium–high. Brush both sides of one gözleme with olive oil. Cook the first gözleme for 3–4 minutes on each side, or until crisp and golden, using a metal spatula to compress it. Cut into wedges and serve immediately, with lots of lemon wedges for squeezing over.

Brush both sides of the second gözleme with olive oil and cook it in the same way, while your guests eat the first.

**FIRED UP
VEGETARIAN**

BUDDHA'S DELIGHT

As the name suggests, there is a link between this dish and Buddha. Buddhist monks are known to be partial to this dish, which traditionally would contain at least ten different types of vegies. In this version I have kept the vegie list down to include those that cook easily and quickly on the barbecue. Feel free to add your favourites, but remember that if you add hard vegies like carrots they'll need parboiling before making it to the barbecue.

Preheat the barbecue grill and hotplate to high.

Pour some of the oil into a large bowl, add the mushrooms and toss to lightly coat. Cook on the grill for 4–5 minutes on each side, or until tender. Remove to a clean bowl and cover to keep warm.

Add a little more oil to the oiled bowl. Add the corn and leek and toss to lightly coat in the oil. Cook on the hotplate for 2–3 minutes on each side, or until tender, then add to the bowl with the mushrooms and cover to keep warm.

Add the remaining oil to the oiled bowl, then lightly coat the bamboo shoots and beans, then the tofu. Add the bamboo shoots and beans to the hotplate, and the tofu to the grill, and cook for 4–5 minutes, or until the bamboo and beans are just tender but crisp, and the tofu is heated through.

Meanwhile, combine all the soy ginger sauce ingredients in a small saucepan, stirring to make sure the cornflour has dissolved. Cook over medium heat until the mixture boils and turns from a thin, cloudy sauce to one that is clear and thickened.

Tumble the warm cooked vegetables onto a serving plate and pour the sauce over. Serve warm.

NOTE: Whole bamboo shoots are generally sold packed in cryovac bags, available from Asian grocers.

60 ml (2 fl oz/¼ cup) rice bran oil
12 large shiitake mushrooms, stems removed
12 Swiss brown mushrooms, stems removed
400 g (14 oz) baby corn, halved lengthways
4 baby leeks, white part only, halved lengthways
100 g (3½ oz) peeled whole bamboo shoots, sliced (see Note)
100 g (3½ oz) green beans, trimmed
300 g (10½ oz) firm tofu, cut into slices 1 cm (½ inch) thick

SOY GINGER SAUCE
125 ml (4 fl oz/½ cup) vegetable stock
1 tablespoon light soy sauce
1 tablespoon finely grated fresh ginger
½ teaspoon sugar
1 teaspoon cornflour (cornstarch)

MUSHROOM BULGOLGI

Serves 4

200 g (7 oz) fresh shiitake
    mushrooms
200 g (7 oz) oyster mushrooms
200 g (7 oz) medium-sized field
    mushrooms
4 pine mushrooms, or 2 large
    king oyster mushrooms,
    thickly sliced
1 teaspoon toasted sesame
    seeds

MARINADE
60 ml (2 fl oz/¼ cup) Korean
    or Japanese soy sauce
1 tablespoon sesame oil
1 teaspoon toasted sesame
    seeds
2 spring onions (scallions), thinly
    sliced on an angle
2 garlic cloves, finely chopped
1 tablespoon finely grated fresh
    ginger

Okay, so bulgolgi is a popular Korean steak recipe, which translates to something like 'fired meat'. With this recipe, the flavour comes from the marinade. I love a good steak myself, but why should meat get all the fun?

Combine the marinade ingredients in a bowl.

    Cut off and discard any large stems from the mushrooms. Lay the mushrooms in a large, flat dish, pour the marinade over and turn to coat. Cover and refrigerate for 3 hours, or overnight, turning the mushrooms every now and then.

    Remove the mushrooms from the fridge 30 minutes before cooking to bring them to room temperature.

    Preheat the barbecue grill to medium.

    Use tongs to shake the excess marinade off the mushrooms, then arrange them on the grill. Cook the mushrooms, turning them often, for 10–15 minutes, or until dark, tender and aromatic.

    Serve warm, sprinkled with the sesame seeds.

**FIRED UP
VEGETARIAN**

LIME & TURMERIC TOFU STEAKS WITH FRESH SAMBAL

Serves 4

The real flavour in this recipe comes from the sambal, and as far as flavours go, you won't be left wanting. Sambal is a chilli-based condiment used throughout South-East Asia. It is generally cooked, but this is a very raw, very fresh and very tasty version.

Combine the sambal ingredients in a bowl and stir until the stock powder has dissolved. Cover and set aside for 30 minutes, or refrigerate overnight.

Cut the tofu into four equal portions. Place in a flat dish in a single layer.

Combine the lime juice, grapeseed oil and turmeric in a bowl and stir until the turmeric has dissolved and the oil is vibrantly coloured. Pour the marinade over the tofu and turn to coat all over. Set aside for 30 minutes.

Preheat the barbecue grill to high.

Cook the tofu for 2–3 minutes on each side, or until heated through and slightly crusty. Serve warm, with the sambal spooned over and lime cheeks on the side.

600 g (1 lb 5 oz) firm tofu
60 ml (2 fl oz/¼ cup) lime juice
60 ml (2 fl oz/¼ cup) grapeseed oil
¼ teaspoon ground turmeric
lime cheeks, to serve

SAMBAL
1 teaspoon vegetable stock (bouillon) powder
2 kaffir lime leaves, thinly sliced
2 lemongrass stems, pale part only, finely chopped
2 bird's eye chillies, finely chopped
3 tablespoons finely chopped red Asian shallots
2 garlic cloves, finely chopped
1 tablespoon vegetable oil
1 tablespoon lime juice

71

BIG PLATES

GRILLED PUMPKIN GNOCCHI WITH GREEN CHILLI CREAM

Serves 4

½ butternut pumpkin (squash),
    about 1 kg (2 lb 4 oz), or
    you can use the top end
    of a larger pumpkin
95 g (3¼ oz/½ cup) fine semolina,
    plus extra for sprinkling
2 tablespoons finely grated
    parmesan cheese, plus
    extra to garnish
1 egg, lightly beaten
rice bran oil, for brushing
flat-leaf (Italian) parsley,
    to garnish

GREEN CHILLI CREAM
250 ml (9 fl oz/1 cup) thin
    (pouring) cream
1 large green chilli, split down
    the middle
25 g (1 oz/¼ cup) finely grated
    parmesan cheese

The idea for this tasty number stems from Roman gnocchi, which is baked and cut into larger pieces than the little 'pillow' gnocchi we are familiar with.

Preheat the barbecue hotplate to medium.

Wrap the pumpkin in two layers of foil. Sit the whole pumpkin on the hotplate. Cook for 1 hour, turning the pumpkin over every 20 minutes, until firm when pierced with a skewer or knife. Remove from the heat and allow the pumpkin to cool in the foil.

Preheat the oven to 180°C (350°F/Gas 4).

Unwrap the pumpkin, scoop out the seeds and discard. Scoop the tender pumpkin flesh into a bowl — you should have about 2–2½ cups. Mash well, then stir in the semolina, parmesan and egg until smooth.

Lightly grease a 25 x 8 x 5 cm (10 x 3¼ x 2 inch) high loaf (bar) tin with oil. Sprinkle a little of the semolina over the base and sides. Spoon the mixture into the loaf tin and bake for 25–30 minutes, or until just set. Remove from the oven, cool to room temperature, then refrigerate until cold.

To make the green chilli cream, put the cream and chilli in a saucepan. Cook over low heat until the cream simmers, but does not boil up. Now simmer for 10 minutes, or until thickened. Stir the parmesan through, then pour into a serving jug or thermos to keep warm.

Preheat the barbecue grill to high. Cut the gnocchi mixture into 12 slices, about 2 cm (¾ inch) thick. Brush each of the cut sides with oil. Cook on the grill for 2–3 minutes on each side, or until golden and heated through — don't be tempted to move the gnocchi before they do so easily, or they will stick to the grill.

Arrange the gnocchi on a platter. Drizzle with the warm green chilli cream and serve scattered with parsley and extra parmesan.

72

PANEER & TOMATO SKEWERS

Serves 6

Paneer is a fresh, lightly pressed Indian 'cheese', though not really a cheese in the same sense as many of us would think, as it doesn't have a setting agent like rennet. Like haloumi, it grills well. It can be cubed or cut into steaks and cooked until golden.

Soak 12 bamboo skewers in cold water for 30 minutes.

Meanwhile, combine the dressing ingredients in a bowl and set aside for the flavours to infuse.

Preheat the barbecue hotplate to high. Lightly brush with olive oil.

Alternately thread two pieces of paneer and two cherry tomatoes onto each skewer. Sprinkle with the cumin and fennel seeds.

Lay the skewers on the hotplate and cook for 8–10 minutes, turning often, until the paneer is golden and the tomatoes softened.

Arrange on a serving platter and drizzle with the dressing. Serve warm, with lemon cheeks for squeezing over.

olive oil, for brushing
400 g (14 oz) paneer, cut into
    2.5 cm (1 inch) cubes
24 cherry tomatoes
1 teaspoon cumin seeds
1 teaspoon fennel seeds
lemon cheeks, to serve

HERB & CHILLI DRESSING
1 large red chilli, thinly sliced
    on an angle
60 ml (2 fl oz/¼ cup) light
    olive oil
1 teaspoon sea salt
1 cup roughly chopped coriander
    (cilantro) leaves
1 cup roughly chopped mint
    leaves
2 tablespoons lemon juice

75

BIG
PLATES

JAPANESE VEGETABLE & GINGER PANCAKES

Serves 2

75 g (2½ oz/½ cup) plain
    (all-purpose) flour
250 ml (9 fl oz/1 cup) vegetable
    stock
2 eggs
2 teaspoons finely grated
    fresh ginger
125 g (4½ oz/1 cup) thinly sliced
    spring onions (scallions)
150 g (5½ oz) shiitake
    mushrooms, stems
    discarded, caps thinly sliced
150 g (5½ oz/2 cups) finely
    shredded Chinese cabbage
rice bran oil, for brushing
Japanese mayonnaise, to serve
pickled ginger, to serve
nori flakes mixed with toasted
    sesame seeds, for sprinkling

These are called okonomiyaki, which translates to 'cook your own' or 'cook it yourself'. Which is what barbecuing is all about, right?

So tasty and easy to make, they're a really great vegetarian barbecue meal on their own. Many of the recipes here are for sharing, and you could indeed share these pancakes. But I imagine them to be enjoyed like a barbecued steak — as a solo barbecue eating experience, with nothing more than a few extra tasty bits on the side.

Put the flour in a bowl. Combine the stock and eggs in another bowl and whisk until well combined. Add the stock mixture to the flour and whisk until smooth. Stir in the ginger, spring onion, mushroom and cabbage.

Preheat the barbecue hotplate to medium and brush with oil.

Using one level cupful of the mixture for each omelette, measure four level cupfuls onto the grill to make four omelettes, gently patting them down with a spatula into rough circles about 13–15 cm (5–6 inches) across. Spoon any remaining mixture equally over the omelettes.

Cook for 5 minutes, or until a golden crust starts to form around the edges. Use a large spatula to flip the omelettes over. Cook for another 5 minutes.

Serve warm, with Japanese mayonnaise, pickled ginger, and mixed nori flakes and sesame seeds on the side as condiments.

**FIRED UP
VEGETARIAN**

SPANISH EGG POTS

I've been making these Spanish eggs at my café for years now. It is the most simple brunch dish, and very tasty — even easier if you make the tomato mixture a day ahead.

Heat the olive oil in a saucepan over medium heat. Add the onion and cook for 2–3 minutes, or until the onion softens. Add the capsicum and stir-fry together, then stir the tomato and parsley through. Season to taste with salt and freshly ground black pepper.

Bring to the boil and cook for 8–10 minutes, or until the tomato mixture is thick. (You can cool and refrigerate the mixture at this stage, and reheat just before using, although I prefer to use it straight away.)

Preheat the barbecue grill or hotplate to high.

Sit four 375–500 ml (13–17 fl oz/1½–2 cup) heatproof dishes on the barbecue to heat up. Spoon about 1 cup of the mixture into each dish and let it get bubbling hot. Use a spoon to make a hollow in the middle of each one, then crack an egg into each dish.

Cover each dish with foil or a small plate and cook for 3–4 minutes, or until the egg whites are firm and the yolks are soft.

Serve hot, with a sprinkling of parsley and a drizzle of extra virgin olive oil, with warm chargrilled bread on the side.

2 tablespoons olive oil
1 red onion, sliced into thin wedges
45 g (1½ oz/¼ cup) thinly sliced roasted red capsicum (pepper) strips
800 g (1 lb 12 oz) tin chopped tomatoes
3 tablespoons finely chopped flat-leaf (Italian) parsley, plus extra to garnish
4 eggs
extra virgin olive oil, for drizzling
chargrilled bread, to serve

81

BIG PLATES

WHOLE BAKED RICOTTA WITH WARM TOMATO & OLIVE SALSA

Serves 6-8

olive oil, for brushing
1 kg (2 lb 4 oz) fresh ricotta
1 teaspoon sea salt

TOMATO & OLIVE SALSA
60 ml (2 fl oz/¼ cup) olive oil
24 small truss cherry tomatoes,
    preferably still on the vine
4 thyme sprigs
2 garlic cloves, finely chopped
80 ml (2½ fl oz/⅓ cup) sherry
    vinegar
50 g (1¾ oz/½ cup) small
    black olives, pitted and
    roughly chopped
60 g (2¼ oz/⅓ cup) small salted
    capers, well rinsed
3 tablespoons finely chopped
    flat-leaf (Italian) parsley

I have used one of my favourite barbecuing tricks here: by laying a sheet of baking paper on the grill or hotplate, you can cook ingredients that might otherwise get stuck. You can also then use the baking paper to tip the cooked ingredients into a bowl or directly onto a serving plate.

Preheat the barbecue grill or hotplate to high.

Tear off a large sheet of foil and place it on a work surface. Lay a similar-sized piece of baking paper over the foil. Lightly brush the paper with olive oil to grease it.

Tip the ricotta out onto the baking paper and sprinkle with the salt. Bring the sides of the foil up to enclose the ricotta, pressing the foil over to seal the ricotta inside. Sit the parcel on the grill or hotplate and cook for 10 minutes, or until the ricotta is heated through. Leave wrapped to keep it warm while making the salsa.

To make the salsa, pour 1 tablespoon of the olive oil into a bowl. Add the tomatoes and thyme and toss to lightly coat the tomatoes in the oil. Tear off a sheet of baking paper and lay it on the hotplate. Tumble the mixture onto the baking paper and cook for 3-4 minutes, until the tomatoes have softened.

Carefully pick up the baking paper sheet by the corners and tumble the tomatoes into a bowl. Add the remaining salsa ingredients. Season to taste with sea salt and freshly ground black pepper and stir well to combine.

Spoon the salsa over the warm ricotta and serve.

**FIRED UP
VEGETARIAN**

TOFU, TOMATO & SHIITAKE SKEWERS WITH GINGER & SPRING ONION DRESSING

Serves 4

You could try using silky, soft tofu here, but it does tend to stick to the hotplate and break up easily. One way to avoid this is to put some baking paper on the hotplate. I generally prefer soft tofu, but am using the firm variety in this recipe, simply because it looks better when it makes it to the table.

Soak eight bamboo skewers in cold water for 30 minutes.

To make the dressing, put the ginger and spring onion in a small heatproof bowl. Heat the oil in a small saucepan over high heat until smoking hot. Pour the hot oil over the ginger and spring onion so they sizzle and soften, then stir in the soy sauce and sesame oil. Set aside while preparing the skewers.

Cut the tofu into pieces about the same size as the tomatoes.

Randomly thread some tofu, three tomatoes and three mushrooms on each skewer. Put the skewers in a flat dish or on a plate. Combine the oil and soy sauce and brush the mixture over the vegies and tofu.

Preheat a barbecue hotplate to high. Cook the skewers for 8 minutes, turning every couple of minutes, until golden and tender.

Spoon the dressing over the skewers. Serve scattered with coriander sprigs.

NOTE: The ginger and spring onion dressing can be made a day in advance. Store it in an airtight container in the fridge until needed and bring back to room temperature before using.

300 g (10½ oz) firm tofu
24 truss cherry tomatoes
24 small shiitake mushrooms
1 tablespoon rice bran oil
2 teaspoons light soy sauce
coriander (cilantro) sprigs,
    to garnish

GINGER & SPRING
ONION DRESSING
2 tablespoons julienned
    fresh ginger
125 g (4½ oz/1 cup) thinly sliced
    spring onions (scallions)
60 ml (2 fl oz/¼ cup) rice bran oil
2 tablespoons light soy sauce
1 teaspoon sesame oil

83

BIG PLATES

BIG MUSHROOMS WITH MARINATED FETA

Serves 4

2 thyme sprigs
2 garlic cloves, sliced
2 spring onions (scallions),
    finely sliced on an angle
125 ml (4 fl oz/½ cup) light
    olive oil
½ teaspoon sea salt
2 tablespoons sherry vinegar
200 g (7 oz) semi-soft goat's
    feta cheese
8 large field mushrooms, or
    pine mushrooms if available
1 teaspoon sumac (see Notes
    on page 19)
finely chopped flat-leaf (Italian)
    parsley (optional), to garnish

I would say the top two vegies to cook on the barbecue are eggplant (aubergine) and mushrooms. They lend themselves to all sorts of cooking styles and pair well with many different flavours. I have made my own herb-infused oil here, but if you can get your hands on soft feta marinated in oil with garlic and herbs, then by all means use that. All you'll then have to do is spoon the ready-marinated cheese into the mushroom caps and cook them on your barbecue. Very nice.

Put the thyme, garlic and spring onion in a heatproof bowl.

Heat the olive oil in a small frying pan over medium heat. When the oil is smoking hot, pour in the spring onion mixture, allowing it to sizzle in the oil and release the flavours. Stir in the salt, vinegar and some freshly ground black pepper to taste.

Cut the feta into small bite-sized cubes and arrange in a flat non-metallic dish. Spoon the spring onion mixture over the feta. Cover and marinate in the refrigerator for up to 3 days.

Preheat the barbecue grill to high.

Remove the stems from the mushrooms and spoon some pieces of feta and the marinade into the caps. Sit the mushrooms on the grill, then close the barbecue lid, or cover the mushrooms with a baking tray. Cook for 15 minutes, or until the mushrooms are tender.

Serve warm, sprinkled with the sumac, and parsley if desired.

**FIRED UP
VEGETARIAN**

FLAVOURS-OF-INDIA PIZZA

Serves 4

Have you ever tried freshly made naan bread? It's pretty good, but not an easy thing to whip up at home. Well, not for most of us anyway.

I wouldn't suggest that we only ever cook with ready-made items, but they do have their place. Convenience is one thing, and some of the packet naan breads out there are okay if they are reheated — so using them for a pizza base seems only logical. And tasty.

Preheat the barbecue grill to medium.

Combine the passata, fennel, cumin, chilli flakes and salt in a small bowl.

Sit each naan bread on a double-thickness sheet of baking paper — this will make it easier to lift the pizzas on and off the barbecue grill. Spread the tomato mixture over each naan bread. Randomly scatter the zucchini, capsicum and onion over the top, then scatter with the paneer.

Put the pizzas on the grill, then close the barbecue lid if you have one, or cover the pizzas with a baking tray. Cook for 10 minutes. Lift up the pizzas with a metal spatula to see how they are cooking underneath, just like they do with wood-fired pizzas — a toasty golden brown base is what you are looking for.

Scatter with coriander leaves and serve warm, with lime pickle on the side.

250 ml (9 fl oz/1 cup) tomato passata (puréed tomatoes)
½ teaspoon fennel seeds
½ teaspoon ground cumin
½ teaspoon chilli flakes
½ teaspoon sea salt
4 naan breads or roti, each about 15 cm (6 inches) long
1 zucchini (courgette), very thinly sliced
1 small red capsicum (pepper), thinly sliced
1 small red onion, very thinly sliced
100 g (3½ oz) paneer cheese, roughly crumbled
coriander (cilantro) leaves, to garnish
lime pickle, to serve

MISO BROWN RICE IN LOTUS LEAVES

Serves 4

2 large dried lotus leaves
(available from Asian grocers)
1 tablespoon white miso paste
2 tablespoons light soy sauce
1 teaspoon sesame oil
½ teaspoon sea salt
½ teaspoon sugar
2 tablespoons rice bran oil
2 garlic cloves, finely chopped
1 tablespoon finely grated
fresh ginger
2 spring onions (scallions),
finely chopped
75 g (2½ oz/1 cup) finely
shredded Chinese cabbage
75 g (2½ oz/1 cup) finely
shredded bok choy (pak choy)
or choy sum
200 g (7 oz/1 cup) long-grain
brown rice, cooked until
tender, then drained

What started as a small plate option turned very quickly into a big one: it was so tasty I couldn't stop eating it! I then realised how full I was afterwards — another good sign, given all the good-for-you things in this dish.

The lotus leaves are a yum cha (or dim sum) inspiration, where it is used as a parcel for sticky rice. Here's another great way to use these aromatic leaves.

Dried lotus leaves are usually folded in half; don't unfold them or they will break. Lay them in the kitchen sink and pour over enough boiling water to cover. Leave for 1 hour, so they become tender and turn the colour of fresh grape vine leaves. Remove the leaves from the water. Unfold the leaves and cut in half, removing any stem. Trim each half into 30 cm (12 inch) squares and set aside.

Combine the miso, soy sauce, sesame oil, salt and sugar in a jug. Pour in 125 ml (4 fl oz/½ cup) boiling water and stir well to make sure all the miso has dissolved.

Heat the rice bran oil in a frying pan or wok over high heat. Add the garlic, ginger and spring onion and stir-fry for a few seconds, or until aromatic but not burning. Add the cabbage and bok choy and stir-fry for 5 minutes, or until well wilted.

Add the rice and the miso mixture. Stir to combine, then bring to the boil. Reduce the heat to medium and cook for 5 minutes, or until almost all the liquid has been absorbed.

Lay the four lotus leaf squares on a work surface. Spoon one-quarter of the rice mixture into the centre of each. Roll the leaves up to make firm parcels.

Preheat the barbecue hotplate to medium.

Sit the parcels on the hotplate, seam side down, and cook for 10 minutes, until the seam side looks dry and blistered. Turn them over and cook for another 5 minutes. Serve warm.

88

ZUCCHINI, EGGPLANT & HALOUMI SKEWERS

Serves 4

Haloumi is one of those ingredients that seemed to appear from out of nowhere to become one of my favourite things to cook. Here it is cubed and skewered with eggplant and zucchini. You could also slice the haloumi into 'steaks' about 1 cm (½ inch) thick, marinate them in a mixture of chilli flakes, dried oregano, olive oil and lemon juice, then cook on the grill until a golden crust forms. Serve with couscous, if desired.

500 g (1 lb 2 oz) haloumi cheese
2 Japanese eggplants
   (aubergines)
2 zucchini (courgettes)
2 tablespoons olive oil, plus
   extra for brushing
2 tablespoons apple cider
   vinegar
2 teaspoons cumin seeds
1 teaspoon chilli flakes
baby rocket (arugula) leaves,
   to serve

Soak eight bamboo skewers in cold water for 30 minutes.

Cut the haloumi, eggplant and zucchini into 2 cm (¾ inch) chunks. Alternately thread two bits of haloumi onto each skewer with some eggplant and zucchini. Lay the skewers on a flat dish.

Mix the olive oil, vinegar, cumin and chilli in a small bowl, then pour the mixture over the skewers. Cover and set aside at room temperature for a couple of hours for the flavours to infuse.

Preheat the barbecue hotplate to high. Brush with a little olive oil to lightly grease.

Put the skewers on the hotplate, reserving the marinade in the dish, and cook for 2–3 minutes, or until a dark-golden crust has formed on the haloumi.

Use a metal spatula to turn the skewers over, then cook for another 2 minutes.

Scatter lots of rocket on a serving plate and pile the skewers alongside. Drizzle with the reserved marinade and serve.

91

**BIG
PLATES**

FRAGRANT FIVE-SPICE VEGETABLE PARCELS

Serves 4

12 medium-sized shiitake
    mushrooms, stems removed
1 small sweet potato, cut into
    rounds 1 cm (½ inch) thick
200 g (7 oz) peeled daikon, cut
    into 3 cm (1¼ inch) cubes
200 g (7 oz) firm tofu, cut into
    2 cm (¾ inch) pieces
2 tablespoons thinly sliced shiso
    leaves (see Note)
60 ml (2 fl oz/¼ cup) good-quality
    soy sauce
1 tablespoon mirin
½ teaspoon sugar
½ teaspoon Chinese five-spice
1 teaspoon sesame oil

Shiitake mushrooms have such a wonderful savoury aroma. Dried shiitakes are even more intense and also work well for this recipe. They store well, are inexpensive and easy to use. Just pour over boiling water to cover and leave to soften for about 30 minutes, then discard the stems and either use the caps whole or chop them up. This dish is great served with steamed brown rice.

Preheat the barbecue hotplate to high.

Combine all the ingredients in a large bowl. Tear off a sheet of foil about 30 cm (12 inches) square and place a similar-sized piece of baking paper over the foil.

Spoon a quarter of the vegie mixture in the middle of the baking paper. Bring the sides of the foil up to enclose the vegetables, sealing the edges together. Repeat to make four parcels.

Sit the parcels on the hotplate and cook for 12–15 minutes, or until the vegetables are tender and aromatic. Serve hot.

NOTE: Also known as perilla, and related to mint, shiso is a herb with round, serrated green or purplish leaves. If you can't get any, use flat-leaf (Italian) parsley instead.

92

GADO GADO WITH SATAY SAUCE

Gado gado, literally meaning 'mix mix', is one of the first exotic things I remember eating. Up there with lumpia (Indonesian spring rolls), this dish was what we dined on during our Indonesian language class excursions. Traditionally, this recipe would use fresh or uncooked ingredients. This version uses grilled vegies, topped off with the satay sauce. And, really, is there anything better than a good satay sauce?

To make the satay sauce, put the peanuts and vegetable oil in a frying pan over medium heat. When the peanuts start to sizzle, cook for another 2–3 minutes, or until golden, then pour into a metal colander set over a heatproof bowl.

Discard the oil and put the hot peanuts in a food processor with the garlic, chilli and sugar. Whiz until a thick paste forms, then scrape the mixture into a saucepan. Stir in the coconut milk and kecap manis and bring to the boil. Reduce the heat to very low and cook for 20 minutes, or until the mixture is very thick.

Preheat the barbecue grill and hotplate to high.

Combine the zucchini, eggplant and capsicum in a large bowl, and the beans and onion in another bowl. Add the rice bran oil to both bowls and toss the vegies around so they are all evenly coated in the oil.

Cooking in batches, tumble the zucchini, capsicum and eggplant over the grill, and spread the beans and onions over the hotplate (these are best cooked on the hotplate as they will tend to fall through the grill bars). Cook for 10–15 minutes, removing the vegetables as they become golden and tender; some will cook more quickly than others. Put the cooked vegies in a bowl and cover to keep warm while the rest are being cooked.

Season the vegetables with sea salt and freshly ground black pepper and pile them onto a serving plate. Top with the bean sprouts. Spoon the satay sauce over, or serve it on the side.

2 zucchini (courgettes), thickly sliced on an angle

1 eggplant (aubergine), thickly sliced

1 red capsicum (pepper), cut into thick strips

200 g (7 oz) green beans or flat beans

2 small red onions, cut into thick wedges, keeping the roots intact

2 tablespoons rice bran oil

115 g (4 oz/1 cup) bean sprouts

SATAY SAUCE
125 g (4½ oz) raw peanuts
1½ tablespoons vegetable oil
1 garlic clove, chopped
1 small red chilli, chopped
1½ tablespoons light brown sugar
400 ml (14 fl oz) coconut milk
1 tablespoon kecap manis

95

BIG PLATES

NAKED SAMOSAS

Serves 4

4 medium-sized russet (idaho)
    or king edward potatoes
2 tablespoons light olive oil,
    plus extra for brushing
½ teaspoon black mustard seeds
1 onion, thinly sliced
1 garlic clove, finely chopped
2 teaspoons finely grated fresh
    ginger
½ teaspoon cumin seeds
1 teaspoon fennel seeds
75 g (2½ oz/½ cup) frozen peas,
    thawed
¼ teaspoon ground turmeric
2 teaspoons sea salt
¼ teaspoon chilli powder
½ teaspoon garam masala
½ cup finely chopped coriander
    (cilantro) leaves and stalks,
    plus extra leaves, to garnish
mango chutney, to serve
plain yoghurt, to serve

So called because they have no pastry. These samosas are more like vegetable patties or burgers, with all the tasty flavours of Indian cooking. You could serve them as a take on a vegie burger — put the samosa on a piece of warm grilled naan bread and top with chutney, yoghurt and coriander.

Peel and wash the potatoes. Cut each into eight pieces and place in a saucepan. Cover with cold water, bring to the boil and cook for 15 minutes, or until just tender. Drain well, then tip the potatoes out onto a clean chopping board to cool and dry.

Put the potatoes in a large bowl and roughly mash them.

Heat the olive oil in a frying pan over high heat. Add the mustard seeds and cook until the seeds start to pop. Add the onion and cook, stirring, for 4–5 minutes, or until golden. Now add the garlic, ginger, cumin seeds and fennel seeds and stir-fry for 1 minute, until aromatic. Mix the peas through.

Pour the onion mixture over the potatoes. Add the turmeric, salt, chilli powder, garam masala and coriander. Stir together using a large spoon, making sure the ingredients are really well combined. Cover and set aside at room temperature for an hour or two for the flavours to develop, or refrigerate until needed.

Using slightly wet hands, divide the mixture into eight equal portions, then form into balls. Gently pat down into discs or patties.

Preheat the barbecue hotplate to high. Brush with a little olive oil to lightly grease.

Cook the patties on the hotplate for 10 minutes on each side, or until they have a golden crust.

Serve warm, garnished with coriander leaves, with chutney and yoghurt on the side.

**FIRED UP
VEGETARIAN**

FAT POLENTA CHIPS WITH EGGPLANT, TOMATO & FRESH MOZZARELLA

Serves 4

I've been making these killer polenta chips for years now. The simple trick is using two types of polenta: fine and coarse. It might seem overly fussy, but try these and you'll probably agree they're the best you've ever eaten.

Line a 25 x 8 x 8 cm (10 x 3¼ x 3¼ inch) loaf (bar) tin with plastic wrap.

Bring the stock to the boil in a saucepan over high heat.

Combine the fine and coarse polenta in a bowl. Pour the polenta into the boiling stock, whisking continuously until smooth and well combined. Reduce the heat to low and stir with a wooden spoon for just a minute, until the mixture is completely smooth. Stir in the parmesan, butter and caraway seeds.

Scrape the mixture into the loaf tin and smooth the top with the back of a spoon. Chill for several hours, or overnight, until cold.

Turn the polenta out onto a chopping board. Cut the polenta crossways into 12 thick slices.

Preheat the barbecue grill to high.

Put the eggplant and onion in a bowl with a splash of rice bran oil. Season with sea salt and freshly ground black pepper and toss to lightly coat. Spread the vegies on the grill, so they don't overlap, and cook for 8–10 minutes, turning often, until golden and tender.

Transfer the vegies to a bowl, add the parsley and chilli and toss to combine. Cover and set aside while cooking the polenta.

Brush the polenta with some oil and cook on the grill for 3–4 minutes on each side, or until grill marks are well formed.

Arrange layers of the polenta, eggplant and tomato on a serving platter. Roughly tear the mozzarella and scatter over the top. Drizzle with olive oil, garnish with basil leaves and serve.

875 ml (30 fl oz/3½ cups) vegetable stock
125 g (4½ oz) fine quick-cooking polenta
125 g (4½ oz) coarse quick-cooking polenta
50 g (1¾ oz/½ cup) finely grated parmesan cheese
25 g (1 oz) unsalted butter, chopped
½ teaspoon caraway seeds
1 small eggplant (aubergine), sliced into thick rounds
1 red onion, sliced into thick rounds
rice bran oil, for coating
3 tablespoons roughly chopped flat-leaf (Italian) parsley
1 large red chilli, finely chopped
2 heirloom tomatoes, sliced
extra virgin olive oil, for drizzling
200 g (9 oz) buffalo mozzarella cheese
basil leaves, to garnish

101

BIG PLATES

CHAKCHOUKA

Serves 4

///

60 ml (2 fl oz/¼ cup) rice bran oil
6 ripe tomatoes, cut in half
1 small yellow capsicum
    (pepper), cut into strips
1 small green capsicum (pepper),
    cut into strips
1 small red capsicum (pepper),
    cut into strips
1 red onion, cut into rings
1 large red chilli, finely chopped
1 teaspoon ground cumin
1 teaspoon sweet paprika
1 teaspoon sea salt
8 eggs
3 tablespoons finely chopped
    flat-leaf (Italian) parsley
chargrilled bread, to serve

Translating Arabic to English can be tricky. That is why, in the world of food, you often see the names of Middle Eastern dishes spelt in different ways, as with this fabulously flavoursome dish from North Africa.

This must be the vegetarian equivalent to bacon and eggs as hangover food. The name alone makes you want to sit up and take notice.

Preheat the barbecue grill to high.

Put the oil in a large bowl. Add the tomatoes, capsicums and onion and toss the vegies around to coat them in the oil.

Working in batches, tumble some of the vegies over the grill and spread them around so they don't overlap. Cook the vegetables for 8–10 minutes, turning them often using metal tongs until they are tender and scored with grill marks, then transfer to a bowl. Cook the remaining vegetables in the same way.

Sprinkle the cooked vegetables with the chilli, cumin, paprika and salt and toss together. Lightly mash using a potato masher, so the tomatoes especially are well crushed. Spoon the mixture onto a heavy-based baking tray. Put the tray on the barbecue grill and allow to heat up and sizzle.

Form eight evenly spaced little wells in the mixture, then crack an egg into each one.

Close the barbecue lid, if your barbecue has one, or place another baking tray over the top. Cook for 8–10 minutes, just until the egg whites are firm. Sprinkle with the parsley and serve hot, with chargrilled bread.

102

**FIRED UP
VEGETARIAN**

MUSHROOMS WITH MANCHEGO RAREBIT

Serves 4

Manchego is a Spanish cheese, not unlike cheddar. This dish is a hybrid of a fondue and Welsh rarebit. Again, as with the other mushroom recipes, feel free to substitute other varieties — so long as they're not tiny!

125 ml (4 fl oz/½ cup) beer
200 g (7 oz/2 cups) grated
  manchego cheese
olive oil, for brushing
12 medium-sized field
  mushrooms
flat-leaf (Italian) parsley sprigs,
  to garnish
smoked paprika, for sprinkling

Preheat the barbecue hotplate to medium.

Combine the beer and cheese in a small saucepan. Cook over medium heat, stirring until the mixture is smooth. Sit the saucepan on a warm part of the barbecue to keep the mixture gooey.

Lay a sheet of baking paper on the hotplate and lightly brush with olive oil to grease it. Sit the mushrooms, gill side down, on the baking paper. Cook for 8–10 minutes, or until tender.

Turn the mushrooms over, then spoon the rarebit into the caps. Close the barbecue lid, or cover the mushrooms with a baking tray. Cook for 5 minutes, until the cheese has melted and the mushrooms are tender.

Serve hot, garnished with parsley and sprinkled with paprika.

SIDES & SALADS

These recipes are about flavour and colour. And lots of it. Side dishes and salads might be considered support acts, but occasionally they can be called upon to star as a starter dish.

Few things are better than sliced summer tomatoes splashed with olive oil and sea salt. But this is a barbecue recipe book, after all, and as much as I love a simple tomato salad, I also love using a barbecue to cook food.

The barbecue is used year round in my house. Rain is about the only thing to stop me, but even then I am lucky enough to have a large, sheltered verandah from which to barbecue.

And year-round barbecuing means that non-summer vegies are not overlooked. So, I make the most of late summer eggplant (aubergine), beans in spring, root vegies and leeks in autumn. Even grilled fruits like figs and peaches can make a sweet salad addition when tossed with some bitter lettuce leaves, nuts and cheese.

Have a tangy, vinegar-spiked dressing on hand to douse over hot grilled vegies so they soak up all that flavour. Remember, salads aren't just for summer. Rug up in the cooler months and enjoy some hearty and comforting vegies, hot off the barbecue.

GRILLED CAULIFLOWER WITH VINEGAR & GARLIC DRESSING

Serves 4–6

1 small cauliflower, about 1 kg
    (2 lb 4 oz)
2 tablespoons rice bran oil

VINEGAR & GARLIC DRESSING
1 tablespoon finely chopped
    garlic
60 ml (2 fl oz/¼ cup) light olive oil
1 teaspoon smoked Spanish
    paprika
½ cup roughly chopped flat-leaf
    (Italian) parsley
1 teaspoon sea salt
60 ml (2 fl oz/¼ cup) red wine
    vinegar

If you are thinking it is odd to cook cauliflower on the barbecue then I would have to agree. I'm no huge fan of cooking 'hard' vegies on the barbecue, but the method used here works nicely. The cauliflower is first parboiled, rendering it tender. The barbecue then heats it up just enough to warmly bring out all the flavours of the Spanish-inspired dressing.

To make the dressing, put the garlic in a heatproof bowl. Heat the olive oil in a small saucepan over high heat. When smoking hot, pour the oil over the garlic so it sizzles, softens and infuses the oil. Before the garlic browns, quickly stir in the paprika, parsley and salt, then add the vinegar. Set aside to infuse.

Cut the cauliflower into large florets, then in half lengthways. Bring a large saucepan of water to the boil and add the cauliflower. When the water returns to the boil, remove the pan from the heat and drain the cauliflower well. Toss the cauliflower in a large bowl with the rice bran oil and a little sea salt.

Preheat the barbecue grill or hotplate to high. Tumble the cauliflower over the barbecue and cook for 2–3 minutes on each side, or until lightly golden.

Return the cauliflower to the bowl and pour the dressing over. Leave for at least 30 minutes for the tasty flavours to infuse the cauliflower, turning occasionally.

Turn the cauliflower in the dressing again before serving.

**FIRED UP
VEGETARIAN**

ISRAELI EGGPLANT SALAD

Serves 4

If you're ever looking for a decent reference book on cooking vegies, try to get your hands on a copy of Mollie Katzen's *The Enchanted Broccoli Forest*. In the eighties it was in the kitchen of just about every other student. It is a well-worn book on my shelf and was the inspiration for this delicious recipe.

Preheat the barbecue grill to high.

Sit the eggplants and tomatoes on the grill. When they start to smoke, give them a turn. Continue until the vegies look charred all over, then remove from the grill.

When cool enough to handle, peel the eggplant skins and discard — there's no need to be too fussy about removing all the burnt bits as these add flavour. Tear the flesh of the eggplant into long lengths and place in a bowl.

Peel and discard the skins of the tomatoes. Chop the flesh and add it to the eggplant, along with any seeds and juice. Don't mix them together at this stage.

Put the dressing ingredients in a bowl and stir to combine. Pour the dressing over the vegetables and use a large spoon to gently coat all the vegies — you don't want to break them up too much. Stir the herbs through and season well.

Serve warm, or at room temperature, garnished with extra parsley.

2 eggplants (aubergines)
4 truss tomatoes
1 cup coriander (cilantro) leaves
1 cup chopped flat-leaf (Italian) parsley, plus extra leaves, to garnish

DRESSING
60 ml (2 fl oz/¼ cup) olive oil
60 ml (2 fl oz/¼ cup) lemon juice
2 teaspoons ground cumin
2 teaspoons hot paprika
½ teaspoon cayenne pepper

SIDES & SALADS

SWEET & SOUR PUMPKIN

Serves 6

1 small jap or kent pumpkin
   (winter squash)
2 tablespoons rice bran oil

DRESSING
80 ml (2½ fl oz/⅓ cup) red
   wine vinegar
60 ml (2 fl oz/¼ cup) olive oil
2 garlic cloves, finely chopped
¼ teaspoon chilli flakes
2 teaspoons soft brown sugar
1 cup mint leaves, roughly
   chopped
40 g (1½ oz/¼ cup) currants

Sweet and sour is not a flavour combination unique to Chinese cooking. The Sicilians are masters too, albeit in a much more subtle way. The combination of sugar and vinegar is common in southern Italian cooking.

Cut the pumpkin in half using a large knife. Scoop out the seeds with a large metal spoon and discard. Lay the cut side of the pumpkin flat on a chopping board. Cut the pumpkin into thick wedges, following the natural indentations.

Place the pumpkin in a bowl with the rice bran oil, season well with sea salt and freshly ground black pepper and toss to coat.

Combine the dressing ingredients in a bowl, mix well to dissolve the sugar, then set aside.

Preheat the barbecue hotplate to medium.

Lay the pumpkin wedges on the hotplate, cut side down, and cook for 10 minutes. Turn the pumpkin over and cook for another 5–10 minutes, until just tender — you want the pumpkin pieces to retain some firmness so they don't break up too much.

Place the hot pumpkin in a large bowl. Pour the dressing over, toss to combine, then season to taste.

Serve warm, or at room temperature.

112

FIG SKEWERS WITH ROCKET, PARMESAN & POMEGRANATE SALAD

Serves 4

90 g (3¼ oz/2 cups) baby rocket (arugula) leaves

2 tablespoons extra virgin olive oil

8 firm, ripe figs

1 tablespoon pomegranate molasses

50 g (1¾ oz/½ cup) shaved parmesan cheese

3 tablespoons fresh pomegranate seeds

2 lemons, cut into slices 3 cm (1¼ inches) thick

Figs come and go, which is what makes them so special. I have tried all sorts of tasty treats with figs this season.

As a sweet treat, I serve ripe figs with sweetened, orange-flavoured mascarpone, with almonds and organic honey. For a savoury option, simply halve, skewer and chargrill the figs and top with light shavings of good parmesan cheese.

Soak four bamboo skewers in cold water for 30 minutes.

Preheat the barbecue grill to high.

Toss the rocket and olive oil in a bowl and season to taste with sea salt and freshly ground black pepper. Scatter the rocket on a serving plate.

Cut the figs in half and thread four halves onto each skewer. Brush the figs with the pomegranate molasses. Spread the skewers on the grill and cook for 5–6 minutes, turning often, until golden and caramelised.

Arrange the skewers on a large serving plate. Top with the parmesan and pomegranate seeds.

Serve warm, with the lemon slices for squeezing over.

114

FIRED UP VEGETARIAN

THE MUST-HAVE GRILLED VEGIE SALAD

This is a very simple, very tasty recipe to have in your repertoire. Start with a few basics: chopped garlic, chilli, parsley, some sort of oil and something with a tang factor (like vinegar or lemon juice), then just add whatever barbecued vegies you like.

In summer I am partial to vine vegies — eggplant, tomatoes and beans.

1 kg (2 lb 4 oz) roma (plum) tomatoes, halved lengthways
2 large eggplants (aubergines), cut into large chunks
500 g (1 lb 2 oz) green beans
2 red onions, cut into thin rings

DRESSING
4 garlic cloves, finely chopped
2 large red chillies, finely chopped
1 cup roughly chopped flat-leaf (Italian) parsley
125 ml (4 fl oz/½ cup) olive oil
60 ml (2 fl oz/¼ cup) sherry vinegar
1 teaspoon sea salt

Combine the dressing ingredients in a bowl and set aside to infuse.

Preheat the barbecue hotplate and grill to high.

Tumble the tomatoes over the hotplate — avoid cooking them on the grill as they will stick. Spread the eggplant around the grill. Depending on the size of your barbecue, you may need to cook the vegies in batches. Don't overcrowd the barbecue, and make sure the vegies don't overlap — they'll cook better this way. Keep turning the vegies until they are tender and golden.

Put the cooked vegies in a large bowl. While they're still warm, spoon some of the dressing over them, but don't stir the vegies or they'll break up.

Cook the beans and onions on the barbecue in the same manner. When all the vegies are cooked and in the bowl, pour the remaining dressing over.

Tip the salad onto a serving platter. Serve at room temperature.

TANGY SWEET POTATO SALAD

There are some ingredients that, when used with a light hand, give warmth to a dish. Caraway is one of them. Use it sparingly, like fennel seeds, and you will be left wondering what the flavour is exactly. But it doesn't matter, it just tastes very good.

1 medium-sized sweet potato, sliced into rounds 5 mm (¼ inch) thick
2 tablespoons rice bran oil
1 teaspoon caraway seeds
2 dill pickles, finely chopped
3 tablespoons roughly chopped mint leaves
1 large red chilli, finely chopped
2 tablespoons apple cider vinegar
60 ml (2 fl oz/¼ cup) extra virgin olive oil
1 teaspoon caster (superfine) sugar

Preheat the barbecue grill to medium.

Put the sweet potato, rice bran oil and caraway seeds in a bowl and toss to coat the sweet potato well.

Tumble the sweet potato over the grill, then use tongs to spread them out so they don't overlap. Cook for 8–10 minutes on each side, or until caramelised and tender.

Place the hot sweet potato in a bowl. Add the dill pickles, mint and chilli. In a small bowl, combine the vinegar, olive oil and sugar, then drizzle the mixture over the sweet potatoes, gently stirring to combine. Set aside for 30 minutes for the flavours to infuse.

Season to taste with sea salt and freshly ground black pepper and serve.

SPICED PARSNIPS

Serves 4-6

3 tablespoons light olive oil
1 teaspoon ground turmeric
1 teaspoon fennel seeds
1 teaspoon cumin seeds
¼ teaspoon chilli powder
1 teaspoon sea salt
1 kg (2 lb 4 oz) medium-sized
   parsnips
3 tablespoons torn mint leaves
lemon wedges, to serve

Parsnips may seem an odd thing to barbecue, but I barbecue them in winter, when they are abundant and well priced. This vegie needs to be parboiled beforehand, otherwise it will burn before it is cooked through.

In a large bowl, combine the olive oil, turmeric, fennel seeds, cumin seeds, chilli powder and salt.

Bring a saucepan of water to the boil. Peel the parsnips and cut in half lengthways, then add them to the boiling water and cook for 4-5 minutes, or until just starting to soften. Drain well.

Tip the warm parsnips into the bowl with the spiced oil and toss to coat. Cover and set aside at room temperature for 1 hour.

Preheat the barbecue hotplate to high.

Keeping the bowl near the barbecue, lift the parsnips out, letting the excess spiced oil drip back into the bowl, and reserving the spiced oil. Tumble the parsnips over the hotplate and spread them out so they don't overlap.

Cook the parsnips for 5 minutes on each side, or until tender and slightly charred. Drizzle the reserved spiced oil over the parsnips and cook for just a few more seconds.

Transfer to a serving plate and season with sea salt and freshly ground black pepper to taste. Scatter with the mint.

Serve warm, with lemon wedges.

120

**FIRED UP
VEGETARIAN**

BOLD POTATOES

Those who know even a little Spanish will probably recognise this as patatas bravas, a much bastardised dish. Potatoes are not supposed to be eaten cold and wrinkled. Cold is fine, but not wrinkled too, which is how this dish is done by the lazy chef — even though it is actually less effort to make these splendid potatoes live up to their name.

These are very good enjoyed with a glass of rosé or some Spanish beer.

4 large boiling potatoes,
    such as desiree, scrubbed
    but not peeled
60 ml (2 fl oz/¼ cup) olive oil
1 teaspoon sea salt
1 cup roughly chopped flat-leaf
    (Italian) parsley

SAUCE
250 ml (9 fl oz/1 cup) tomato
    passata (puréed tomatoes)
85 g (3 oz/⅓ cup) good-quality
    mayonnaise
2 garlic cloves, crushed
2 tablespoons white wine vinegar
1 teaspoon smoked paprika
1 teaspoon ground cumin
1 teaspoon chilli flakes

Combine the sauce ingredients in a bowl. Season to taste with sea salt and freshly ground black pepper. Cover and set aside for the flavours to develop while cooking the potatoes.

Preheat the barbecue hotplate to medium.

Cut the potatoes into slices no thicker than 5 mm (¼ inch). Place in a bowl, add 1 tablespoon of the olive oil and the salt, then toss around to evenly coat the slices in the oil.

Tumble the potatoes over the hotplate and use tongs to spread the slices out so they don't overlap. Close the lid, if your barbecue has one, and cook for 10 minutes, or until golden. (If your barbecue doesn't have a lid, just cook the potatoes a little longer at a slightly lower temperature.)

Turn the potato slices over, close the lid and cook for another 5–6 minutes, or until golden and tender.

Spread the sauce down the middle of a long serving plate. Tumble the potatoes over, scatter with the parsley and drizzle with the remaining olive oil. Serve hot.

123

SIDES &
SALADS

POOR MAN'S POTATOES

Serves 6–8

1 kg (2 lb 4 oz) new potatoes,
   cut in half
2 red onions, thickly sliced
2 green capsicums (peppers),
   thickly sliced
4 garlic cloves, finely sliced
2 bay leaves
3 tablespoons roughly chopped
   flat-leaf (Italian) parsley
60 ml (2 fl oz/¼ cup) olive oil
60 ml (2 fl oz/¼ cup) white wine
1 teaspoon smoked paprika
1 teaspoon sea salt
good-quality mayonnaise,
   to serve

I love titles like this. They come from a time when people were so much more snobby and classist about who ate what. And if you ate potatoes you were considered poor! But how good are potatoes, fried into chips, mashed with cream, slow-cooked in a curry... or baked in foil with a few aromatics, as they are here.

Tear off two large sheets of foil, about 30 cm (12 inches) long. Tear off two sheets of baking paper about the same size, then rinse the paper under cold water and wring out the excess water. The baking paper will look like crumbled fabric. Lay the damp paper on the foil.

Preheat the barbecue hotplate to medium. Close the lid of the barbecue to create a hot oven effect. (If your barbecue doesn't have a lid, simply cook the potatoes at a lower temperature, and for slightly longer than the times given below.)

Put all the ingredients, except the mayonnaise, in a clean plastic bag. Hold the bag shut and shake vigorously to make sure all the ingredients are really well combined. Tumble the contents of the bag onto the baking paper. Bring the edges of the foil together and twist to enclose the potato mixture, so it looks like a giant dumpling. Secure the foil with kitchen twine or wooden pegs.

Sit the foil bag on the barbecue, close the lid and cook for 20 minutes. Use a clean cloth to grab the top of the foil bag and gently shake so the flavours are well combined and coat the potatoes. Turn the bag over and cook for a further 15 minutes, or until the potatoes are tender.

Serve the potatoes warm or at room temperature, with a dollop of mayonnaise.

124

**FIRED UP
VEGETARIAN**

LEMON SOY GRILLED ONIONS

Serves 4

Chargrilled onions smell so wonderfully appetising when cooked on the barbecue. In Australia, onions may well be the vegetable that most people associate with barbecued food! Here the humble onion is combined with some simple flavours for a super-tasty result.

Preheat the barbecue grill to high.

Put the onions and oil in a bowl and toss to coat. Tumble the onions over the grill and sprinkle with the salt. Use tongs to spread them around so the onions don't overlap. Cook, turning often, for 10–15 minutes, or until golden and tender.

Transfer the onions to a serving plate. Combine the soy sauce, lemon juice and mirin in a bowl, then pour the mixture over the onions while they are still warm.

Sprinkle with the spice powder and serve.

NOTE: Also known as Japanese seven-spice, shichimi togarashi is a zesty spice mixture containing ground red chillies, sesame seeds, ginger and seaweed, commonly sprinkled over soup, noodles and fried foods. It's widely sold in Asian supermarkets and spice shops.

4 white onions, thickly sliced
2 tablespoons rice bran oil
1 teaspoon sea salt
60 ml (2 fl oz/¼ cup) tamari (Japanese soy sauce)
60 ml (2 fl oz/¼ cup) lemon juice
1 tablespoon mirin
1 teaspoon shichimi togarashi (see Note)

125

SIDES & SALADS

BARBECUED CORN WITH HOT SALSA

Serves 4

4 fresh corn cobs
60 ml (2 fl oz/¼ cup) melted
    butter
35 g (1¼ oz/¼ cup) finely grated
    parmesan cheese

SALSA
2 tablespoons olive oil
1 tablespoon lime juice
3 tablespoons finely diced
    roasted piquillo peppers or
    red capsicum (pepper)
3 tablespoons chopped jalapeño
    chillies, in brine, drained
½ cup roughly chopped coriander
    (cilantro) leaves and stalks
2 spring onions (scallions), thinly
    sliced

I had a corn recipe in my original *Fired Up* barbecue book, which proved to be really popular. It involved serving barbecued corn with butter, lime juice and parmesan cheese. Using parmesan here may sound a little odd, but it really adds an extra savoury element — something the Japanese call 'umami'.

Combine all the salsa ingredients in a large bowl and set aside.

Preheat the barbecue hotplate to high.

Brush the corn cobs with some of the melted butter, sit them on the hotplate and cook for 8–10 minutes, turning and brushing with more melted butter every couple of minutes, until the corn is starting to char around the edges.

Transfer the corn cobs to a plate. Season well with salt and freshly ground black pepper and sprinkle with the parmesan.

Serve warm, with the salsa on the side.

126

FIRED UP
VEGETARIAN

GRILLED EGGPLANT WITH CHIPOTLE LABNEH

Serves 4–6

Labneh is a slightly tangy soft cheese made from salted and strained yoghurt, widely enjoyed for breakfast in the Middle East. As it has increased in popularity it is much easier to get your hands on these days. Try it once and you will appreciate its deliciousness!

If you can't find labneh, don't despair: it is very easy to make yourself. For every cup of natural yoghurt, stir through 1 teaspoon salt. Spoon it into some clean cloth, such as muslin (cheesecloth), and firmly tie to enclose the yoghurt in the cloth. Suspend it over a bowl so the water drips out, then refrigerate overnight. The next day, have a look in the cloth and you will see labneh.

Put the chipotle labneh ingredients in a food processor and whiz until just combined, leaving some flecks of chilli. Set aside.

Preheat the barbecue grill to high.

Cut the eggplant lengthways down the middle, then cut each piece crossways in half. Place in a bowl, drizzle with the rice bran oil and toss to coat the eggplant.

Tumble the eggplant over the grill, using tongs to spread the pieces out so they don't overlap. Cook, turning often, for 10–15 minutes, or until golden all over.

Place the eggplant in a bowl. Add the garlic, lemon juice and herbs and toss together while the eggplant is still hot.

Tumble the eggplant onto a serving plate. Drizzle with olive oil and serve with thick dollops of the chipotle labneh.

NOTE: Chipotle chillies are often packed in adobo — a spicy red chilli sauce. You'll find them packed in tins and jars in spice shops and good food stores.

2 small eggplants (aubergines), no more than 15 cm (6 inches) long
2 tablespoons rice bran oil
1 garlic clove, crushed
2 tablespoons lemon juice
3 tablespoons roughly chopped mint leaves
3 tablespoons roughly chopped flat-leaf (Italian) parsley
extra virgin olive oil, for drizzling

CHIPOTLE LABNEH
2 whole smoked chipotle chillies in adobo sauce, plus 1 tablespoon of the sauce (see Note)
300 g (10½ oz) labneh

SICILIAN GRILLED VEGETABLE SALAD

Serves 4–6

2 medium-sized eggplants
    (aubergines)
1 small cauliflower
1 tablespoon light olive oil

DRESSING
125 ml (4 fl oz/½ cup) olive oil
2 tablespoons red wine vinegar
2 garlic cloves, crushed
1 cup roughly chopped mint
1 cup roughly chopped flat-leaf
    (Italian) parsley leaves
1 cup basil leaves, torn
2 tablespoons small salted
    capers, rinsed and drained
½ teaspoon sugar
45 g (1¾ oz/¼ cup) raisins

I'm using eggplant and cauliflower here, but you could also use zucchini (courgette), broccolini and capsicum (pepper). Any vegie will do, really, so long as you add the dressing to the just-cooked vegetables, letting them soak up all the tasty bits — kind of like a reverse marinade.

Combine all the dressing ingredients in a large bowl.

Preheat the barbecue grill to medium.

Slice the eggplants into 1 cm (½ inch) rounds, and cut the cauliflower into bite-sized florets. Put them in a bowl with the olive oil, season well with sea salt and freshly ground black pepper and toss to coat.

Tumble the eggplant and cauliflower over the grill and spread them out so they don't overlap. Cook for 8–10 minutes, then turn them over and cook for another 5 minutes, or until just tender.

Put the hot vegetables in a large bowl, pour the dressing over and toss to combine. Cover with plastic wrap and set aside at room temperature for at least 30 minutes or up to 1 hour, allowing all the flavours to infuse.

Toss together, season to taste and serve.

**FIRED UP
VEGETARIAN**

SUGAR PUMPKIN WITH LENTILS & TANGY DRESSING

Serves 4

It would not be the first or last time I have used the following technique to make a dressing or a sauce. Gently heating aromatics in some oil teases out the flavours and infuses these through the oil. And don't be afraid of lentils — they are tender, tasty and good for you.

To make the dressing, put the olive oil, chilli and garlic in a small saucepan over medium heat. When the chilli and garlic start to sizzle, cook for just a minute or two longer, then remove from the heat. Stir in the vinegar, sugar and salt and mix until dissolved. Pour into a jar or bowl and set aside to infuse.

Put the lentils in a small saucepan and pour in enough water to cover. Bring to the boil, then reduce the heat and simmer until the lentils are tender but not mushy — this may take as little as 5 minutes, or up to 20 minutes, depending on the age of your lentils, so check them regularly. Drain well and set aside.

Preheat the barbecue grill to medium.

Cut the pumpkin in half, then scoop out and discard the seeds. Leaving the skin on, cut the pumpkin into wedges no thicker than 2 cm (¾ inch). Brush the flesh with the rice bran oil and cook on the grill for 10 minutes on each side, or until golden and cooked through, checking regularly to ensure it doesn't burn too much.

Put the hot pumpkin in a large bowl with the onion, herbs and lentils. Stir the dressing, then pour it over the pumpkin.

Toss gently to combine. Serve warm.

55 g (2 oz/¼ cup) puy lentils
  or tiny blue-green lentils
1 sugar or butternut pumpkin
  (squash), about 2 kg
  (4 lb 8 oz)
1 tablespoon rice bran oil
1 red onion, finely sliced
1 cup small mint leaves
1 cup flat-leaf (Italian) parsley
  leaves

TANGY DRESSING
60 ml (2 fl oz/¼ cup) light
  olive oil
1 large red chilli, finely sliced
4 garlic cloves, finely sliced
60 ml (2 fl oz/¼ cup) white
  wine vinegar
2 tablespoons sugar
½ teaspoon sea salt

SIDES & SALADS

INDIAN SPICED EGGPLANT

Serves 4–6

2 medium-sized eggplants
    (aubergines)
2 tablespoons rice bran oil
3 teaspoons sea salt
2 tablespoons olive oil
1 garlic clove, crushed
1 teaspoon ground cumin
½ teaspoon chilli powder
125 g (4½ oz/½ cup) labneh
    (strained yoghurt cheese;
    see introductory notes on
    page 129)
1 cup mint leaves, roughly torn

Take note of this method of adding seasoning and flavour to just-cooked eggplant. The heat of the eggplant releases the fragrant oil in the spices. Eggplant is a highly absorbent vegie — you'll notice how much oil it sucks up when being fried.

Preheat the barbecue grill to medium.

Cut the eggplants lengthways into large wedges. Place in a bowl with the rice bran oil and salt and toss to coat in the oil. Tumble the eggplant onto the grill and cook for 12–15 minutes, using tongs to spread the wedges out and to turn them often, until golden and just tender. Transfer to a bowl.

Combine the olive oil, garlic, cumin and chilli powder in a small bowl. Pour the dressing over the eggplant while it is still hot, then gently toss to coat in the spice mixture.

Pile the eggplant onto a serving platter. Serve warm, scattered with the mint, with the labneh on the side.

CHARGRILLED PANEER & SPINACH SALAD

Serves 4

What you're after here is the salad all ready to go in a bowl. To this you are going to toss through warm, golden, just-cooked cubes of paneer and a simple dressing. The warm paneer will soften the spinach and entice the flavours from the dressing.

Preheat the barbecue grill or hotplate to high.

Combine the spinach, tomatoes, spring onion and coriander in a large bowl and set aside.

Pat the paneer dry with paper towels and cut into 2 cm (¾ inch) cubes. Place in a bowl, drizzle with a little olive oil and toss to coat. Put the paneer cubes on the grill or hotplate and cook for about 8 minutes, turning often so each side is golden.

Add the warm cheese to the spinach mixture, along with the cumin, olive oil and lemon juice. Season to taste with sea salt and freshly ground black pepper and toss to combine.

Serve the salad while the cheese is still warm.

200 g (7 oz) baby English spinach leaves
200 g (7 oz) small teardrop tomatoes, halved
2 spring onions (scallions), thinly sliced on an angle
½ cup roughly chopped coriander (cilantro) leaves
200 g (7 oz) block paneer (Indian cottage cheese; see introductory notes on pages 38 and 75)
2 tablespoons olive oil, plus extra for drizzling
1 teaspoon ground cumin
2 tablespoons lemon juice

139

BALINESE GRILLED EGGPLANT WITH TOMATO SAMBAL

Serves 4

2 eggplants (aubergines)
vegetable oil, for brushing
lime wedges, to serve

SAMBAL
4 ripe tomatoes
4 garlic cloves, unpeeled
2 red Asian shallots, unpeeled
1 vegetable stock (bouillon) cube,
    preferably gluten free
1 small red chilli
¼ teaspoon ground white pepper
2 tablespoons soft brown sugar

Sambal is to Bali and Indonesia what harissa is to Morocco. This is an unadulterated chilli sauce — hot, spicy and with a real kick. It is added to curries and used as a condiment in its own right with grilled meats.

Preheat the barbecue grill to high.

To make the sambal, sit the tomatoes, garlic and shallots on the grill and cook for 8–10 minutes, turning often and removing each vegetable from the grill when they are charred all over. Remove from the heat until cool enough to handle, then peel all the vegies and discard the skins.

Put the garlic flesh in a food processor with the tomatoes, shallots, crumbled stock cube, chilli, pepper and sugar. Whiz together until smooth, then pour the mixture into a small saucepan and simmer for 10 minutes, or until slightly thickened. Transfer to a bowl and allow to cool.

Preheat the barbecue grill to medium.

Cut each eggplant in half lengthways and make several shallow, diagonal incisions on the flesh side of the eggplant. Brush the cut side with oil. Place on the grill, cut side down, and cook for 8–10 minutes, or until golden and charred around the edges.

Turn the eggplant over and cook for another 5 minutes, or until it has collapsed and is soft.

Serve the eggplant warm, with some sambal spooned over, and lime wedges on the side.

140

**FIRED UP
VEGETARIAN**

CHARGRILLED FENNEL WITH CHILLI & HERBS

Serves 4

Fennel in all its forms is delicious. The feathery tops add flavour to dressings and mayonnaise. The beefy bulbs can be cooked in all sorts of ways — in pasta sauces, risotto, minestrone, and roasted with pork or chicken. Fennel seeds are a staple in my cupboard, ready to be used in Indian and Italian-inspired recipes.

4 medium-sized fennel bulbs, preferably with fronds
2 garlic cloves, chopped
3 tablespoons olive oil
2 tablespoons red wine vinegar
2 teaspoons dijon mustard
½ teaspoon sea salt
chilli flakes, to taste
1 cup flat-leaf (Italian) parsley leaves, finely chopped
1 cup mint leaves, finely chopped

If the fennel has feathery fronds, cut these off and roughly chop up enough to give a small handful. Set aside.

Slice the fennel lengthways into slices 5 mm (¼ inch) thick. Place in a bowl with the garlic and 1 tablespoon of the olive oil. Set aside at room temperature for 30 minutes to infuse.

In a large bowl, combine the remaining olive oil with the remaining ingredients to make a herb dressing.

Preheat the barbecue grill to high.

Tumble half the fennel over the grill and spread the slices out so they don't overlap. Cook for 4–5 minutes on each side, until the fennel is golden and charred and the garlic is golden and aromatic. Add the hot fennel to the herb dressing and toss to coat.

Cook the remaining fennel in the same manner and toss it through the dressing. Serve warm or at room temperature, sprinkled with any reserved fennel fronds.

BARBECUED BEANS WITH MISO DRESSING

Serves 4

300 g (10½ oz) green beans
1 tablespoon rice bran oil
½ teaspoon black sesame seeds

MISO DRESSING
3 tablespoons white miso
1 teaspoon caster (superfine) sugar
2 tablespoons sake
1 teaspoon tamari (Japanese soy sauce) or light soy sauce
½ teaspoon sesame oil

Beans are seasonal, which makes them extra special. They are pricey when sold pre-packed in small portions at the local fruit and veg store. If you venture out to a farmers' market you will pick up a box of them for a fraction of the price. This miso dressing is great with grilled eggplant (aubergine) too.

You can trim any woody ends off the beans, but I prefer to leave them intact.

Place all the miso dressing ingredients in a food processor and whiz to combine. With the motor running, add 60 ml (2 fl oz/¼ cup) hot water, so the mixture turns paler and more creamy in colour. Set aside while cooking the beans.

Preheat the barbecue hotplate to high.

Toss the beans in a bowl with the oil until lightly coated.

Tumble the beans over the hotplate, then use tongs to spread them out so they don't overlap. Cook for 4–5 minutes, turning every minute or so, until the beans are nicely browned and tender around the edge.

Pile the beans into a bowl and sprinkle with the sesame seeds. Spoon the miso dressing over, or serve it on the side.

144

FIRED UP VEGETARIAN

CHARGRILLED LEEKS WITH HOT MUSTARD MISO DRESSING

Serves 4

It's best to use baby leeks here if you can, simply because they are novel and very seasonal. Otherwise, the big fellas will do, but they will need longer on the barbecue and they may need a good bath beforehand.

Preheat the barbecue grill to high.

Wash the leeks well to remove any dirt from the roots. Rinse and drain well, then place the leeks on a tray. Add the oil and salt and toss to coat well.

Combine the dressing ingredients in a small bowl, using a fork to mash the miso and to whisk together until lump-free.

Cook the leeks on the grill for 8–10 minutes, or until golden and tender, turning them every now and then.

Lay the leeks on a serving plate and pour the dressing over. Serve warm, sprinkled with the sesame seeds.

16 baby leeks, untrimmed
2 tablespoons rice bran oil
1 teaspoon sea salt
2 teaspoons toasted sesame seeds

HOT MUSTARD MISO DRESSING
2 tablespoons white miso paste
2 teaspoons hot English mustard
2 tablespoons tamari (Japanese soy sauce)
2 tablespoons rice vinegar

147

SIDES & SALADS

POTATOES IN FOIL WITH HERBED LABNEH

Serves 4

4 large potatoes, with skin on, washed

HERBED LABNEH
125 g (4½ oz/½ cup) labneh
1 tablespoon finely snipped chives
1 tablespoon finely chopped flat-leaf (Italian) parsley
1 tablespoon finely chopped mint

Go and get some labneh (see introductory note on page 129) and try it, please. And use it in all kinds of dishes, as a substitute for all sorts of other things. Try it in dips instead of sour cream. Use it as you would hummus — or yoghurt, which is what it is anyway. You can even use labneh to replace ricotta or cream cheese in sweets such as cheesecake.

Combine the ingredients for the herbed labneh in a bowl and mix together well. Cover and set aside at room temperature, or refrigerate until needed.

Preheat the barbecue hotplate to medium.

Wrap each potato in foil. Sit them on the hotplate, then close the barbecue lid, or cover the potatoes with a large stainless steel bowl or baking tray. Cook for 1 hour, turning often, until the potatoes are tender. You can check if the potatoes are cooked without unwrapping them by pressing on them with tongs or a spatula — when cooked, the potatoes will feel soft.

Remove the potatoes from the hotplate and leave them in their foil wrapping for 10–15 minutes. (You can leave them on the barbecue lid to keep warm.)

Unwrap the potatoes, then press down on them with a spatula to flatten and split the skin.

Spoon the herbed labneh over the hot potatoes and serve.

CHARGRILLED ASPARAGUS WITH DILL & MUSTARD CRÈME FRAÎCHE

Serves 4

This is not reinventing the wheel. Take one tasty, seasonally fresh vegetable — namely, asparagus — cook it simply, then combine it with other tasty classic ingredients. Do choose asparagus when it is in season, and please avoid buying asparagus that has flown a long way on a plane to reach you. That seems just too weird.

Preheat the barbecue grill to high.

Combine all the dill and mustard crème fraîche ingredients in a bowl. Mix together well and set aside.

Snap off and discard the woody ends of the asparagus. Toss the asparagus in a bowl with the olive oil and salt.

Tumble the asparagus over the grill and use tongs to spread the spears out so they don't overlap. Cook, turning often, for 6–8 minutes, or until lightly charred and tender.

Spread the dill and mustard crème fraîche over a large serving platter. Arrange the asparagus on top. Drizzle with olive oil and serve immediately.

24 thin asparagus spears
1 tablespoon light olive oil
½ teaspoon sea salt
extra virgin olive oil, for drizzling

DILL & MUSTARD
CRÈME FRAÎCHE
250 g (9 oz/1 cup) crème fraîche
2 tablespoons good-quality
    whole-egg mayonnaise
2 teaspoons dijon mustard
2 tablespoons finely chopped dill
2 tablespoons finely chopped
    flat-leaf (Italian) parsley
1 tablespoon lemon juice

151

SIDES & SALADS

MIGAS & TOMATO SALAD

Serves 4

60 ml (2 fl oz/¼ cup) milk
4 slices ciabatta bread
olive oil, for drizzling
3 tomatoes, roughly chopped
2 tablespoons red wine vinegar
1 small garlic clove, crushed
½ cup roughly chopped flat-leaf
(Italian) parsley

I'll interpret this in a very broad sense: migas is a dish using leftover bread in Spanish, Portuguese and Mexican cooking. The bread can be soaked in a mixture of milk and water and it is then deep-fried. This is a tasty technique, but impossible to replicate when cooking outside on a barbecue. Cooking the soaked bread on a hotplate is a convenient alternative, if not a bit healthier.

Preheat the barbecue hotplate to high.

Combine the milk and 60 ml (2 fl oz/¼ cup) water in a bowl. Soak each slice of bread in this mixture for 1 minute.

Remove the bread from the milk mixture and gently squeeze out as much liquid as possible. Drizzle the hotplate generously with olive oil and cook the bread for a couple of minutes on each side, until golden and crispy around the edges.

Remove the bread from the hotplate and allow to cool. When cool enough to handle, roughly tear the bread and place in a bowl with the tomato, vinegar, garlic and parsley. Season well with salt and freshly ground black pepper and gently toss to combine.

Serve warm.

FIRED UP VEGETARIAN

SWEET POTATOES IN JACKETS WITH CREAMY FETA

Serves 4

Sweet potato, like potato, cooks up really well on the barbecue, wrapped in foil and cooked until fluffy and soft on the inside, with the skin a little chewy and sweet.

To make the feta and dill cream, put the feta, garlic, dill and olive oil in a food processor and whiz to a thick paste. With the motor running, add the milk, blending until thick and creamy. Set aside.

Cut the pointy ends off the sweet potato, then cut it into four portions about the same size.

Preheat the barbecue hotplate to medium.

Tear off four sheets of foil, large enough to completely wrap each piece of sweet potato. Sit a piece of sweet potato in the centre of each piece of foil. Pour 1 tablespoon of the olive oil over each and sprinkle with the salt. Loosely wrap each portion in the foil and place them on the hotplate.

Close the barbecue lid, or cover the parcels with a baking tray. Cook for 45 minutes, turning often, until the sweet potato is very tender.

Unwrap the sweet potato parcels and spoon the feta and dill cream over while still hot.

1 large sweet potato, peeled
80 ml (2½ fl oz/⅓ cup) olive oil
1 teaspoon sea salt

FETA & DILL CREAM
100 g (3½ oz) soft feta cheese, crumbled
1 garlic clove, crushed
3 tablespoons chopped dill
2 tablespoons olive oil
2 tablespoons milk

153

SIDES & SALADS

CHARGRILLED WITLOF WITH PARSLEY, LEMON & PECORINO

Serves 4

light olive oil, for brushing
8 witlof (chicory), cut in half
    lengthways
1 teaspoon sea salt
1 cup roughly chopped flat-leaf
    (Italian) parsley
2 tablespoons lemon juice
2 tablespoons finely grated
    pecorino cheese

This recipe may well epitomise many of the great things about barbecuing, as well as many of the great things we associate with rustic, Italian cooking. Take a raw ingredient and don't mess with it too much — just grill until golden, sweet and slightly charred, and serve with some herbs, lemon juice and cheese. Nice.

Preheat the barbecue hotplate to medium–high and lightly brush with olive oil.

Sit the witlof, cut side up, on the hotplate. Cook for 5 minutes, or until golden underneath. Turn the witlof over and cook for another 5 minutes, or until tender.

Put the hot witlof in a large bowl with the remaining ingredients. Season with freshly ground black pepper and toss to combine.

Serve warm.

154

BREADS

When serving bread at a barbecue, I prefer those that are best for sharing. In saying this, I realise that any bread can be broken as a symbol for sharing. But with a barbecue I like to serve up breads that literally need to be broken, or torn, to be shared. This is pass-around bread. Break-with-your-hands bread. Scoop-up-something-tasty-with-it bread.

This sort of bread also has the added benefit of avoiding a knife and a chopping board. One less thing to remember at a barbecue is always a good thing.

For these breads I look to Asia, North Africa, the Mediterranean and the Middle East for inspiration. From these places come the flatbreads, pan breads or grilled breads that go best with my style of barbecuing.

These breads can be prepared in very little time, with very little fuss, and with very little knowledge of breadmaking. The traditions and techniques of these breads do not come from artisan bakers, chefs or apprentices, but from homes and homemakers — from family cooks with very basic means, armed only with a pair of hands, a domestic oven and a need to satisfy hunger.

Aside from making bread with ease, I think the most exciting element to these bread recipes is that you end up with something someone else is also enjoying in a place very different from you.

Using ingredients that can be found at any corner store, you can make bread that can be found in the piazzas of Sicily, the derbs of Marrakesh, the tapas bars of Spain or dhabas of India. It's a very universal thing, bread. And these tasty, authentic breads are made to share, and can all be cooked on your very own barbecue.

PALERMO FOCACCIA

Makes 1 loaf

3 teaspoons instant dried yeast
450 g (1 lb/3 cups) strong
    flour, such as '00' flour
2 tablespoons olive oil, plus extra
    for brushing
coarse polenta, for dusting
½ teaspoon sea salt
60 ml (2 fl oz/¼ cup) tomato
    passata (puréed tomatoes)
1 teaspoon dried oregano
extra virgin olive oil, to serve

There are many versions of this bread. This cake-like bread is a common staple in the market places of Palermo, Sicily. Sometimes anchovies are studded into the dough prior to baking, or fresh ricotta is smeared over the top. In situ, this bread looks more like an iced cake. But do push this sweet simile aside: this is a really great-tasting, moreish bread.

Put 60 ml (2 fl oz/¼ cup) warm water in a small bowl. Quickly stir in the yeast and 1 tablespoon of the flour, leaving the mixture lumpy. Cover and leave somewhere warmish and draught-free for 10–15 minutes, or until frothy and spongy-looking.

Brush a round metal baking tin with olive oil — my tin is 23 cm (9 inches) across and 5 cm (2 inches) deep. Sprinkle the base and sides with the polenta.

Put the salt and remaining flour in the bowl of an electric mixer fitted with a dough hook. Add the yeast mixture, olive oil and 250 ml (9 fl oz/1 cup) warm water and knead for 10 minutes, or until smooth and elastic. (Alternatively, mix the dough together, turn out onto a clean work surface and knead the dough by hand for 10 minutes.)

Tip the dough into the greased tin. Dip your fingers in flour and gently press the dough to the sides of the tin, making dimples as you go, and making sure it is an even thickness all over.

Spoon the passata over the dough and sprinkle with the oregano. Leave in a warm, draught-free spot for about 1 hour, or until the dough has risen.

Preheat the barbecue grill to medium–high and close the lid to keep it warm. Put a rack on the grill and sit the focaccia tin on the rack. Close the lid, or cover the focaccia tin with a large stainless bowl. Cook for 15–18 minutes, or until the focaccia is golden around the edges and dry on top. (The bread may need longer cooking time if you are covering it with a bowl.)

Serve warm, with extra virgin olive oil for dipping into, and sea salt for sprinkling over.

POCKET BREADS

These are fun. I am not sure how it actually works, but you end up with a puffed-up, disc-like bread. When cool, it can be split in two and used as a savoury pocket — especially tasty when filled with falafel, hummus, pickled vegies and tangy tzatziki.

2¼ teaspoons instant dried yeast
1 teaspoon sugar
500 g (1 lb 2 oz/3⅓ cups) strong flour, such as '00' flour, plus extra, for dusting
2 teaspoons sea salt

Pour 60 ml (2 fl oz/¼ cup) warm water into a small bowl. Quickly stir in the yeast and sugar — leaving a few lumpy bits is fine. Cover and leave somewhere warmish and draught-free for 10–15 minutes, or until frothy and spongy-looking.

Put the flour and salt in a large bowl. Add the yeast mixture and 250 ml (9 fl oz/1 cup) warm water and use one hand to combine. Tip the mixture onto a floured surface, or into the bowl of an electric mixer fitted with a dough hook. Knead for 15 minutes, or until the dough is smooth and elastic.

Divide the dough into eight equal portions. Shape each piece into a ball, then roll each ball into a disc about 12–15 cm (4½–6 inches) in diameter. Lay the discs on a sheet of floured baking paper, then cover with a cloth and leave in a warm spot for about 1 hour, or until puffed and very soft.

Preheat the barbecue hotplate to high. Close the lid of the barbecue to allow the lid to get really hot.

Working in batches if necessary, put the pitta breads on the hot barbecue lid and leave for 10 minutes. They will start to look dry and puff up, forming that distinctive pitta or pocket-bread shape.

Turn the breads over and put them on a heavy-based baking tray lined with baking paper. Place a rack on the barbecue hotplate and place the tray of pitta breads on top. (You may need to work in batches, depending on the size of your barbecue.) Close the lid and cook, turning often, for 5–8 minutes, or until golden and puffed.

The air inside the breads will be piping hot, so allow the breads to cool a little before serving.

161

BREADS

FLATBREADS WITH PANEER & GREEN CHILLI

Makes 8

300 g (10½ oz/2 cups) plain (all-purpose) flour, plus extra, for dusting
½ teaspoon sea salt
1 teaspoon sugar
½ teaspoon bicarbonate of soda (baking soda)
330 g (11½ oz/1¼ cups) plain yoghurt
2 tablespoons rice bran oil
lemon wedges, to serve

PANEER & GREEN
CHILLI FILLING
1 small red onion, finely chopped
2 long green chillies, finely sliced
2 tablespoons finely chopped coriander (cilantro) leaves and stalks, plus extra leaves, to garnish
100 g (3½ oz) paneer (Indian cottage cheese; see introductory notes on pages 38 and 75), roughly grated

It wasn't until I began researching recipes for this book that I realised how many varieties of bread are actually made in India — breads of different grains, both leavened and unleavened, with or without egg or dairy, oil, spices and even with nuts. I wouldn't say no to any of them.

This bread is a type of kulcha, the sister of naan, made with baking soda rather than yeast. Both naan and kulcha can be served plain, or filled with whatever you like.

Combine the flour, salt, sugar and bicarbonate of soda in a bowl and make a well in the centre. Add the yoghurt to the well and use your hands to combine — the dough will be sticky and wet.

Make another well in the centre and add the oil. Work the oil into the dough until the dough is smooth and shiny. Cover and set aside for 30 minutes, for the yoghurt and soda to react.

Meanwhile, put the filling ingredients in a bowl and combine well.

Form the dough into eight balls, about the size of golf balls. On a lightly floured surface, roll each ball into a flat circle, about 10 cm (4 inches) across. Put one-eighth of the paneer mixture into the centre of each, then bring the sides of the dough together to enclose the filling.

Again, on a lightly floured surface, roll each of the dough rounds into circles no thicker than 5 mm (¼ inch). Place them on a lightly greased sheet of baking paper, then cover with a cloth or plastic wrap. Set aside for about 30 minutes, or until slightly risen.

Preheat the barbecue hotplate to high. Close the lid to create an oven effect.

Using the baking paper, lift the dough rounds onto the hotplate. Close the lid and cook for 3–4 minutes on each side, or until golden and cooked through.

Serve hot, with lemon wedges.

162

BARBARI BREAD

Makes 2 loaves

½ teaspoon sugar
2 teaspoons instant dried yeast
485 g (1 lb 1 oz/3¼ cups) plain
    (all-purpose) flour
1 teaspoon sea salt
1 teaspoon bicarbonate of soda
    (baking soda)
coarse polenta, for dusting
2 tablespoons sesame seeds

TOPPING
½ teaspoon plain (all-purpose)
    flour
½ teaspoon bicarbonate of soda
    (baking soda)

This intriguing bread is the one most commonly eaten in Iran. Its distinctive elements are the parallel lines made in the dough prior to cooking, and the paste of flour, bicarbonate of soda and water that is brushed on top, creating a wonderfully crisp and dry bread. It is very nice with some feta cheese and olive oil.

Combine the sugar, yeast and 60 ml (2 fl oz/¼ cup) warm water in a small bowl. Cover and leave somewhere warmish and draught-free for 10–15 minutes, or until frothy and spongy-looking.

Mix the flour, salt and bicarbonate of soda together in a large bowl. Add the yeast mixture and 310 ml (10¾ fl oz/1¼ cups) warm water and bring together into a sticky dough. Tip onto a floured board and knead for 15 minutes, or until smooth and elastic, or knead in an electric mixer with a dough hook for 10–15 minutes.

Divide the dough into two equal portions. Tear off two large sheets of baking paper, about 40 cm (16 inches) long, and sprinkle with polenta. Place a piece of dough on each sheet, then shape each into a rectangle no more than 1 cm (½ inch) thick. Cover loosely with a cloth and set aside for about 1 hour.

Put the topping ingredients in a small saucepan with 80 ml (2½ fl oz/⅓ cup) water. Cook over medium heat for 1–2 minutes, or until the mixture is thick and cloudy. Allow to cool.

Preheat the barbecue hotplate to high. Sit a baking rack on the hotplate and close the barbecue lid.

Brush the liquid topping over each loaf. Use your fingers to run parallel divots, about 2 cm (¾ inch) apart, down the length of the dough. Sprinkle the sesame seeds over each loaf. Using the baking paper, lift one of the loaves onto a baking tray, then sit the tray on the baking rack. Close the barbecue lid, reduce the heat to medium and cook for 10–15 minutes, or until the base of the bread is dark golden and the top is golden and dry.

Cook the remaining loaf in the same manner. Serve hot.

**FIRED UP
VEGETARIAN**

AFGHANI FLATBREADS

Makes 2 loaves

These are big, rustic, easy-to-make breads. They are really another version of naan, with the option of making them bigger and thinner than the typical naan.

1 tablespoon instant dried yeast
750 g (1 lb 10 oz/5 cups) plain (all-purpose) flour, plus extra for dusting
75 g (2½ oz/⅓ cup) caster (superfine) sugar
1 tablespoon sea salt
60 ml (2 fl oz/¼ cup) rice bran oil or grapeseed oil, plus extra for brushing

Combine the yeast and 60 ml (2 fl oz/¼ cup) warm water in a small bowl. Cover and leave somewhere warmish and draught-free for 10–15 minutes, or until frothy and spongy-looking.

Put the flour, sugar and salt into the bowl of an electric mixer fitted with a dough hook. With the motor running on low, add the yeast mixture, then add 750 ml (26 fl oz/3 cups) warm water, then the oil. Knead for about 10 minutes, or until smooth and elastic. (Alternatively, mix the dough together, turn out onto a clean work surface and knead the dough by hand for 10 minutes.)

Put the dough in a large lightly oiled bowl. Cover and leave for about 1 hour, or until the dough has doubled in size and looks soft and pillow-like.

Divide the dough in half, then roll out each half on a well-floured work surface, into large, flat circles about 20 cm (8 inches) in diameter. Put the dough onto a lightly greased sheet of baking paper, then use your fingers to press the dough all over, making dozens of little divots in the dough.

Preheat the barbecue hotplate to high. Put a baking rack on the hotplate. Use the baking paper to lift one round of dough onto the baking rack. Close the lid of the barbecue to create an oven effect. (If your barbecue doesn't have a lid, cover the dough with a baking tray.) Cook for 10–15 minutes, or until the dough is golden. Brush the top side of the dough with a little oil, flip it over, then cover and cook for another 5 minutes, or until golden on both sides.

Cook the remaining dough in the same manner. Serve warm.

GRILLED GREEN OLIVE BREADS

This is a yeast-free 'bread', and the basic recipe idea hails from northern China. Although, I must admit, the real inspiration comes from Barbara Tropp, a truly passionate and inspiring food writer. This recipe has the interesting technique of using hot and cold water to make the dough, combined with the 'snail' shaping of the dough — resulting in a flaky, unleavened pastry.

Place the olive paste ingredients in a food processor and whiz until a smooth paste forms. Scrape into a bowl, then clean out the food processor bowl.

Put the flour and baking powder in the food processor and whiz to combine. With the motor running, add 80 ml (2½ fl oz/⅓ cup) boiling water, then 80 ml (2½ fl oz/⅓ cup) cold water. As soon as all the water has been added, turn the food processor off and scrape the dough out onto a floured surface.

Knead briefly, until the dough forms into a smooth ball. Cover and set aside at room temperature for about 30 minutes.

Divide the dough into four equal portions. Working one at a time, and leaving the others covered, roll out the dough on a lightly floured work surface, into a 20–25 cm (8–10 inch) circle. Spread one-quarter of the olive paste over the dough. Roll the dough up into a long, thin cigar shape, then coil the dough from one end to make a snail shape, tucking the end in. Repeat with the remaining dough and olive paste.

Now use a floured rolling pin to roll the snails into flat circles, about 15 cm (6 inches) across.

Preheat the barbecue hotplate to medium. (If you are cooking this bread on a grill, you will need to put it in the freezer until firm.)

Drizzle the oil over the hotplate, then sit one bread on top. Cook for 3–5 minutes on each side, turning every minute, until golden and slightly puffed. (If it starts to burn, reduce the temperature to medium–low.) Cook the remaining breads in the same way.

Serve hot, torn or cut into wedges.

300 g (10½ oz/2 cups) plain (all-purpose) flour, plus extra for dusting
2 teaspoons baking powder
2 tablespoons rice bran oil

GREEN OLIVE PASTE
60 ml (2 fl oz/¼ cup) olive oil
1 teaspoon sea salt
50 g (1¾ oz/⅓ cup) pitted large Sicilian green olives
1 garlic clove
15 g (½ oz/½ cup) chopped flat-leaf (Italian) parsley
15 g (½ oz/¼ cup) sliced spring onions (scallions)

169

PIADINI STUFFED WITH MANCHEGO & PARSLEY

Serves 4

450 g (1 lb/3 cups) plain
   (all-purpose) flour
2 teaspoons sea salt
2 tablespoons Spanish vinegar
60 ml (2 fl oz/¼ cup) extra virgin
   olive oil, plus extra, for
   brushing
150 g (5½ oz) manchego cheese,
   coarsely grated
4 tablespoons finely chopped
   flat-leaf (Italian) parsley
1 small red onion, finely sliced
lemon wedges, to serve

Piadini is a type of unleavened Italian flatbread. Its rustic nature lends itself perfectly to rustic flavours: onion, herbs and hard cheeses.

Put the flour and salt in a food processor and whiz to combine. With the motor running, add the vinegar, oil and enough cold water to bring the mixture together into large crumbs — you may need as little as 2 tablespoons cold water, or up to about 6 tablespoons.

Tip the mixture out onto a floured surface and knead for 8–10 minutes, until smooth. Wrap the dough in plastic wrap and set aside in a warmish place while you get everything else ready.

Combine the cheese, parsley and onion in a bowl.

Preheat the barbecue hotplate to high.

Cut the dough into four even portions. Roll each dough portion on a floured surface into a long oval shape, about 40 cm (16 inches) long and 15 cm (6 inches) wide. Brush each round with olive oil.

Sprinkle the cheese mixture over two of the rounds, then top these with one of the other bread rounds to make a sandwich. Press the edges to seal them together.

Cook the piadini on the hotplate one at a time for 4–5 minutes, or until golden and crisp underneath. Flip the bread over and cook for another 3–4 minutes, or until golden.

Cut into wedges, or whatever shapes you prefer. Serve warm, with lemon wedges.

170

**FIRED UP
VEGETARIAN**

REAL GARLIC BREAD

Makes 1 loaf

I say 'real' garlic bread because I am using real ingredients here. Let me explain. The few times that I fine-dined as a kid in the seventies, I vaguely remember garlic bread being special. Now it is often something made with butter substitutes and garlic flakes. When made well, garlic bread is lovely. It is so easy to prepare ahead, ready to throw on the barbecue.

1 sourdough baguette, about
    25–30 cm (10–12 inches) long

GARLIC BUTTER
6 organic garlic cloves
1 teaspoon sea salt
3 tablespoons finely chopped
    flat-leaf (Italian) parsley
125 g (4½ oz) organic unsalted
    butter, at room temperature

To make the garlic butter, put the garlic on a chopping board and sprinkle with the salt. Use a large knife to chop the garlic. Every now and then, use the flat side of the knife to press down on the chopped garlic to crush it even more. Continue until you have a very finely chopped heap of garlic. Stir the garlic and parsley through the butter.

Preheat the barbecue hotplate to medium. Sit a baking rack on the hotplate.

Cut deep slices into the bread, about 2–3 cm (¾–1¼ inches) apart. Spread the garlic butter into the cuts, making sure the exposed bread is evenly covered with the butter.

Completely wrap the bread in foil. Sit the bread on the baking rack, flat side down, and cook for 8–10 minutes.

Serve hot.

DAMPER

Makes 1 loaf

300 g (10½ oz/2 cups) plain
  (all-purpose) flour, plus extra
  for dusting
3 teaspoons baking powder
1 teaspoon sea salt
125 ml (4 fl oz/½ cup) milk
olive oil, for brushing

This bread epitomises Australian bush cookery. Like many good things, it originated out of necessity, created by stockmen on long journeys, from the most basic of ingredients. However, there's still a bit of an art to making damper — a bit like making scones. It might take a few attempts to get the damper looking 'right', but it will always taste good.

Combine the flour, baking powder and salt in a bowl, then make a deep well in the centre.

In another bowl, combine the milk and 125 ml (4 fl oz/½ cup) boiling water. Pour the mixture into the flour and use a fork to quickly combine for a few seconds. Now use one hand to mix the dough — it will be a wet dough, so you may need to add just a fine sprinkling of flour.

When the mixture no longer sticks to the side of the bowl, tip it out onto a lightly floured surface and knead for a minute, until smooth.

Using lightly oiled hands, form the dough into a log about 10 cm (4 inches) wide and 15 cm (6 inches) long.

Lay a large sheet of foil on a work surface and place a similar-sized sheet of baking paper on top. Lightly brush the baking paper with olive oil. Sit the dough at one long end of the baking paper. Loosely roll the paper up, then fold the ends over to loosely enclose the dough. Set aside for 30 minutes.

Preheat the barbecue grill to medium.

Sit the bread on the grill and cook for 10 minutes. Turn it over and cook for another 10–13 minutes, or until the bread makes a hollow sound when tapped and is lightly golden all over.

Allow the damper to cool for a few minutes. Slice and serve while still warm.

174

**FIRED UP
VEGETARIAN**

NAAN

This Indian bread can be flavoured with a whole bunch of ingredients: nuts, dried fruit, herbs. But I like my naan unflavoured so I can really appreciate its simplicity. What I most love to do with this bread is mop up any sauce left over from a curry.

Pour 185 ml (6 fl oz/¾ cup) warm water into a bowl or jug and stir in the yeast. Set aside for a couple of minutes.

Combine the flour, sugar, salt and baking powder in a large bowl. Add the oil and yoghurt and combine with one hand. Add the yeast mixture and continue mixing with one hand to make a wet dough.

Lightly oil your hands, then form the dough into a ball. Place in a bowl, cover and set aside for 3–4 hours, or until the dough has doubled in size.

Lightly oil your hands again and divide the dough into six equal portions. Toss each one in flour to coat, then pull and stretch each piece on a lightly floured surface to make an oval shape about 20 cm (8 inches) long.

Preheat a barbecue grill to high. Sit a large heavy-based baking tray on the grill and give it time to heat. Drizzle over some oil to lightly grease it.

Using an oven mitt, remove the tray from the grill, then carefully lay three of the naan breads on the hot tray. Use the flat side of a knife or the back of a spoon to press the dough into the tray. The dough will start cooking on the hot tray.

Sit the tray back on the hot grill and cook the breads for 4–5 minutes, or until the bread is crisp and golden underneath and the top is puffing up. Turn and cook for another 2–3 minutes, or until golden and cooked through. Keep the breads in a warm place.

Cook the remaining breads in the same manner. Serve warm.

1 teaspoon instant dried yeast
300 g (10½ oz/2 cups) plain (all-purpose) flour, plus extra for dusting
1 teaspoon caster (superfine) sugar
1 teaspoon sea salt
½ teaspoon baking powder
2 tablespoons rice bran oil, plus extra for drizzling
70 g (2½ oz/¼ cup) plain yoghurt

175

CORN GRIDDLE BREADS

Makes 4

150 g (5½ oz/1 cup) plain
    (all-purpose) flour
2 teaspoons baking powder
¼ teaspoon sweet paprika,
    plus extra for sprinkling
½ teaspoon sea salt
1 egg, lightly beaten
185 ml (6 fl oz/¾ cup) milk
125 g (4½ oz/½ cup) creamed
    corn
2 tablespoons melted butter
vegetable oil, for brushing
good-quality mayonnaise,
    to serve
thinly sliced spring onion
    (scallion), to serve

These could be called griddle cakes or even corn fritters. When these breads are kept very flat, I like to use them as I would any soft flatbread — they are soft enough to fold around grilled vegies, or scoop up dips, sauces and mayonnaise. Or you can top them with a simple fried egg or spicy Mexican beans. Yum.

Combine the flour, baking powder, paprika and salt in a bowl, then make a well in the centre.

In another bowl, combine the egg, milk and creamed corn. Pour the mixture into the flour well with the melted butter and use a fork to combine.

Preheat the barbecue hotplate to medium and lightly brush with oil.

Pour or ladle the batter, using about 125 ml (4 fl oz/½ cups) for each griddle bread, onto the hotplate, leaving room between each to expand. You should have enough batter for four griddle breads.

Use the back of the spoon to spread each one out into a circle about 12–15 cm (4½–6 inches) across. Cook for 4–5 minutes, or until bubbles form around the edges.

Flip them over and cook for another 2–3 minutes, or until golden and cooked through.

Serve warm, topped with a dollop of mayonnaise, some spring onion and a sprinkling of paprika.

**FIRED UP
VEGETARIAN**

INDEX

Page numbers in *italics* indicate photographs

181

INDEX

FIRED UP
VEGETARIAN

Published in 2013 by Murdoch Books, an imprint of Allen & Unwin.

Murdoch Books Australia
83 Alexander Street
Crows Nest NSW 2065
Phone: +61 (0) 2 8425 0100
Fax: +61 (0) 2 9906 2218
www.murdochbooks.com.au
info@murdochbooks.com.au

Murdoch Books UK
Erico House, 6th Floor
93–99 Upper Richmond Road
Putney, London SW15 2TG
Phone: +44 (0) 20 8785 5995
Fax: +44 (0) 20 8785 5985
www.murdochbooks.co.uk
info@murdochbooks.co.uk

For Corporate Orders & Custom Publishing contact
Noel Hammond, National Business Development Manager, Murdoch Books Australia

Publisher: Sue Hines
Commissioning publisher: Sally Webb
Designer: Hugh Ford
Photographers: Brett Stevens and Nicky Ryan
Stylists: Matt Page and Sarah O'Brien
Editor: Katri Hilden
Food Editor: Grace Campbell
Home Economic: Sonja Bernyk
Project Editor: Claire Grady
Production Manager: Karen Small

The photographs on pages 26, 59, 60, 65, 74, 78, 90, 98, 104, 113, 121, 127, 131, 137, 142, 149, 155, 165 are by Nicky Ryan, styling by Sarah O'Brien. All other photographs are by Brett Stevens, styling by Matt Page.

Text © Ross Dobson 2013
Design and Photography © Murdoch Books 2013

A cataloguing-in-publication entry is available from the catalogue of the National Library of Australia at www.nla.gov.au.

A catalogue record for this book is available from the British Library.

Printed by 1010 Printing.

IMPORTANT: Those who might be at risk from the effects of salmonella poisoning (the elderly, pregnant women, young children and those suffering from immune deficiency diseases) should consult their doctor with any concerns about eating raw eggs.

OVEN GUIDE: You may find cooking times vary depending on the oven you are using. For fan-forced ovens, as a general rule, set the oven temperature to 20°C (35°F) lower than indicated in the recipe.

MEASURES GUIDE: We have used 20 ml (4 teaspoon) tablespoon measures. If you are using a 15 ml (3 teaspoon) tablespoon add an extra teaspoon of the ingredient for each tablespoon specified.